THE PERSONALITY
OF JESUS

Foreword By Robert Coleman, Author of *Master Plan of Evangelism*

THE PERSONALITY OF JESUS

HOW TO INTRODUCE YOUNG PEOPLE TO JESUS CHRIST AND HELP THEM GROW IN THEIR FAITH

♦ ♦ ♦

Francis E. Clark

Ashley Denton, Editor

(Revised & Updated Edition)

THE PERSONALITY OF JESUS

How to Introduce Young People to Jesus Christ and Help
them Grow in their Faith by Learning How to:

- Start a Youth Group or College Ministry that Reflects
  the Personality of Jesus
- Build Relationships with Adolescents
- Lead Small Groups Effectively
- Train Volunteer Youth Leaders
- Reach Schools with the Gospel
- Be a Christ-Centered Parent to Teenagers and College
  Students

Celebrating the 100th Anniversary of
Francis Clark's, *Christ and the Young People*

Copyright © 2015 by Ashley Denton
Original Copyright (*Christ and the Young People*) © 1916 Fleming H. Revell
Company © 1924 by David C. Cook Publishing Company (Public Domain)

Published in the United States by Smooth Stone Publishing, Fort Collins.
www.smoothstonepublishing.com

ISBN-10 0984916520
ISBN-13 9780984916528

LIBRARY OF CONGRESS CATALOGUING-IN-PUBLICATION DATA

Clark, Francis Edward
Denton, Ashley (Editor)
The Personality of Jesus or How to Introduce Young People to Jesus
Christ and Help them Grow in their Faith by Learning How to Start a
Youth Group or College Ministry that Reflects the Personality of Jesus,
How to Build Relationships with Adolescents, How to Lead Small Groups
Effectively, How to Train Volunteer Youth Leaders, How to Reach
Schools with the Gospel, and How to be a Christ-Centered Parent to
Teenagers and College Students/Francis Clark/Ashley Denton

Library of Congress Control Number: 2015901435
Smooth Stone Publishing, Fort Collins, CO

Francis, Clark, (1851-1927)
Ashley, Denton, 1970
p.   cm.

Includes bibliographical references
1. Religion. 2. Christian Ministry. 3. Discipleship. I. Clark, Francis;
Denton, Ashley. II. Title.

TABLE OF CONTENTS

Introduction by Ashley Denton · · · · · · · · · · · · xi

Foreword by Robert Coleman · · · · · · · · · · · · · xv

Foreword to the Original Edition· · · · · · · · · ·xvii

Preface · xxi

Chapter 1 Why Young People Are Drawn to Jesus? · · · · · ·1

Chapter 2 Jesus Is Authentic ·7

Chapter 3 Approachable ·13

Chapter 4 Humble ·19

Chapter 5 Courageous ·25

Chapter 6 Considerate ·33

Chapter 7 Carefree ·39

Chapter 8 Funny ·47

Chapter 9 Enthusiastic ·55

Chapter 10 Tactful ·63

Chapter 11 An Uncomplaining Hero · · · · · · · · · · · · · · · ·73

Chapter 12 Committed ·79

Chapter 13 Idealistic ·85

Chapter 14 What Do You Think of Jesus? · · · · · · · · · · · · ·91

End Notes ·97

"Young people need someone
who is crazy about them."

– Walter Brueggemann

INTRODUCTION

♦ ♦ ♦

ONE OF THE FIRST YOUTH ministry books ever written was Francis Clark's, *Christ and the Young People*. Clark spent enormous amounts of time with kids. He studied them and discovered that there were certain things that they were drawn to in their adult leaders. His vision was to see the development of a robust youth movement that modeled the personality of Jesus. He was convinced that making his dream a reality would depend on recruiting and then training volunteer youth leaders to have the heart and skills of relational evangelism.

Clark embarked on a study of adolescents in the early 1900s that culminated in a list of some of the most attractive qualities young people were drawn to in their youth leaders. He discovered that all of the qualities young people were most attracted to in their leaders were also personality qualities of Jesus. Francis Clark believed that Jesus was the embodiment of everything that young people longed for. The challenge of every generation is simply to give young people an *accurate* picture of Jesus Christ. Clark believed that if young people could just see the winsome personality of Christ, they would naturally be drawn to him, "like a magnet is to metal."

His book (originally published in 1916) sparked new thinking about the importance of student ministry and the theology behind it. To him, student ministry was all about Jesus Christ. Nothing more. Nothing less.

I cut my teeth in student ministry years ago as a volunteer and staff person in the mission organization of Young Life. Since then I've had the opportunity to encourage and equip volunteer leaders and staff in organizations like Cru, Intervarsity, Navigators, YWAM, and dozens of churches and denominations in over 50 countries. I have become convinced that Francis Clark's ideas profoundly influenced many of the founders of these and other organizations toward a biblical theology of youth evangelism. Yet most people these days don't even know about Clark's book. As a life-long youth worker, when I discovered it, it was like uncovering an ancient treasure.

Working with a variety of parachurch organizations, churches, and church planting movements, I believe a common thread throughout most youth evangelism organizations can be traced back to Clark's theology of the incarnation of Christ and his appeal to young people. As I spend time with student ministry leaders across many different cultures, I believe that in addition to Robert Coleman's *Master Plan of Evangelism* (1963), Francis Clark's book, *Christ and the Young People (1916)* is the best, most cross-culturally relevant book written to date on the theology and practice of student ministry (focusing on students between the ages of 12-25). There are a few books that are so profound that I try to re-read them each year. *Christ and the Young People* is one of them.

The original edition of Clark's book was written 100 years ago, so I have done my best to revise and update Clark's writing into modern language. I also updated the title to: *The Personality of Jesus*. I highly recommend reading the original version, but I felt that the old style of his writing could hinder the wide distribution of his book to a modern audience, so I revised it extensively because his ideas are too important to sit on a shelf collecting dust. My method was to retain each and every idea Clark communicated while translating or paraphrasing it into the most modern English possible (without losing his original meaning). A few paragraphs that were impossible for me to translate to the modern context were moved to the *End Notes*.

Each chapter ends with a list of thought-provoking discussion questions for groups. Clark designed his book to be discussed in a small group setting. He envisioned youth leaders taking *groups of students* through a semester-long study of the life of Jesus. You may want to use the book's 14 chapters as a semester-long Bible study. This book is also an *ideal training tool for volunteer student ministry leaders* who lead middle school, jr. high, high school, and university ministries. It is also a great book for parents.

If you would like to read the original version of the book in its original form (2nd Edition, 1924), you can view it at: http://ashleydenton.com/christ-and-the-young-people. If you would like to get more resources related to international youth and family ministry feel free to visit my blog at: ashleydenton.com.

I hope *The Personality of Jesus* will help you grow in your awe of Jesus. I pray that it will give you a clearer vision for how to filter every aspect of ministry in your church, para-church, or mission organization through the personality of Jesus Christ. May these ideas, from one of the first student ministry books ever written, continue to fuel the spreading fire of youth evangelism around the world for years to come.

Ashley Denton, D.Min
Pokhara, Nepal
December 5, 2014

FOREWORD

◆ ◆ ◆

by Robert E. Coleman
Author of *Master Plan of Evangelism*

JESUS CHRIST IS THE MAGNETISM of the Gospel. Everything about His life and work captivates our imagination. In a real sense, He is the photograph of God in human form. When we see ourselves next to the beauty of His holiness, we can recognize how ugly we are in our sin. Yet at the same time, we see in Him what we want to be like... our true identity.

Flowing through His life, ever drawing us to Him, is a love that will not let us go, even when we have turned to our own way and blasphemed His Name ... a love finally demonstrated on the cross when Jesus accepted our judgment and died for our sin. Why would any one not want to know this man, the Son of God, the dearest lover of every of every human soul?

This book lifts up traits in the character of Christ that inspire us to follow Him. Its charm comes in the simple way that the story unfolds. Questions at the end of each chapter will help you think through lessons learned and make personal applications.

Originally authored by Francis Clark a hundred years ago, Ashley Denton has overhauled the first writing, taking care to update and revise the text to make it more readable for a modern audience of young people. The book will be especially helpful to youth pastors, student ministry leaders and parents.

I heartily commend it to you.

–Robert E. Coleman (Author, *Master Plan of Evangelism*)

FOREWORD TO THE ORIGINAL EDITION

♦ ♦ ♦

*Christ and the Young People: For classes,
youth ministries, and organizations.*

SINCE THE FIRST EDITION OF this little book was published,
youth ministries have greatly multiplied. Youth organizations
are offering more training in the Bible, ethics, citizenship,
missions, and matters of public morality.

Yet the Bible, the fountainhead of our civilization, must
always be the main source of these studies. And even more,
the parts of the Bible that reveal the life, the character and the
teachings of our Lord Jesus Christ, must always have the first
place.

To make this volume more useful as a textbook for exhibit-
ing the character of Jesus as revealed in the Gospels, *a series of
questions on each chapter has been added.* By using these questions

I believe that any intelligent teacher can draw out the thoughts of his students on the great subjects involved, and can impress on them the supreme qualities and principles which the Great Teacher came to reveal.

I believe these principles can also greatly encourage church Bible classes, week-day prayer groups and conference meetings. And by reflecting on these questions, one's personal devotional reading can be greatly enhanced. This book is meant to be read slowly so that you have time for personal reflection about the application of these principles to your own youth ministry.

Hundreds of books could not exhaust this exhaustless subject, but by narrowing our focus, especially those who work with young people, will see the main characteristics of Jesus and why he was so attractive to the young.

By making this book brief and small, my hope is that it will be possible to publish it at a price within the reach of every youth worker and every socio-economic strata of society for private study.

Its brevity also makes it possible to teach these principles to youth leaders in just a few leadership training sessions. Yet the content could also lead to more intensive study if you choose.

When the book was first published it was warmly received by the religious press, and it may not be unfitting to add that the distinguished editor of one of the leading Methodist weekly magazines confessed that it appealed to him so strongly that he read it through in one sitting, though it took him half the night to do so. He then published it, chapter by chapter, in his

widely circulated journal, with words of the highest recom-
mendation. Such unsolicited and unexpected positive reviews
inspire the hope and prayer that this new edition may make
the life and character of Jesus even more convincingly real and
attractive to all its readers, young and old.

Boston, Francis Edward Clark

PREFACE

◆ ◆ ◆

MANY ACCOUNTS OF THE LIFE of Christ have been published over the years. And a multitude of study materials for young people have also been written. I do *not* know, however, of a book that looks at the life of Jesus from the standpoint of how young people might hear and understand the Gospel in their own language. This is what this book, however imperfectly, seeks to do.

Instead of going first to the Scripture to find what Christ did or said that would appeal to young people (as may have been the approach of another author), in preparation for writing this book, I first studied the character, the ideals, the leanings and longings of healthy, normal young people who I had known.

Then I searched the Gospel diligently to see how our Savior's life exemplified these ideals and natural characteristics. There is always a danger in theological study, that one might half-unconsciously make the text fit the characteristics. Yet keeping this danger in mind, and trying to avoid it, I have been surprised (though why should I be?) that in every case the ideals of youth, which, as a rule, are the purest and best of any period of life, are exemplified in the earthly life and teachings of our Lord.

Most young people and many teachers of the young, perhaps, have been as slow as myself in making this discovery. To those people I trust this little book will prove that the best in all of us is only a reflection of the Master's life. And therefore it is possible for us to aspire to be "like him, for we shall see him as he is."

Francis Edward Clark. *Boston, Mass.*

CHAPTER 1

WHY YOUNG PEOPLE ARE DRAWN TO JESUS?

◆ ◆ ◆

JESUS CHRIST APPEALS TO EVERY kind of person, to every kind of group, in every possible state of being. His ability to appeal to all people groups is just one sign of his Divinity. Only God in the flesh could do what he did and still appeal to every generation in every culture, in every era of history.

People are fascinated with famous leaders or teachers because of their charisma or talent. Some people can impress intellectuals; others connect better with the poor or uneducated. Some have a gift for reaching the hearts of kids. And others relate better to older people or those who are suffering. Jesus is unique because he was winsome to *everyone*. The young, the old, the fisherman, the tax collector, the scribe, the rich, the blind beggar, Mary and Martha, and the woman caught in adultery; all heard him and were drawn to him.

While this is all true, I have noticed in the Scriptures that he is especially appealing to young people. Jesus never lived to be an old man. He never even reached mid-life. Yet he knew by personal, earthly experience, as well as by his supernatural wisdom, the joys, the limitations, the temptations, and the dreams of young people. (see John 2:24)

He knows what it is like to grow up. He was a baby, a boy, an adolescent, and a mature adult. He worked in his father's shop just like boys today learn from their fathers or grandfathers how to fix a car, work with tools, or plant a garden. Just like we see little boys today getting a drink from a water fountain, he toddled along with his mother to the water well of Nazareth as soon as he could walk.

Just like adolescents today have to patiently study, learn skills, and wait to set sail out into the world on their own, Jesus spent many years in Nazareth as an adolescent before his official ministry was launched. We need to remember that although Jesus was fully God, he was also fully human. Jesus began his public ministry as a young man. Just like young adults today, he was vigorous, enthusiastic and undoubtedly began to feel a sense of power and achievement that young people naturally feel as they grow up.

Maybe this is exactly why young people are so drawn to Jesus: Because he can relate with them on a human level. Most people these days make a decision to follow Christ between the ages of about 12-20. It is well observed that after this, few people come to Christ. In those adolescent years, kids are asking what the young man asked Jesus: "Good Master, what do I need to do to inherit eternal life?"

It is my aim in this chapter and those that follow to try to introduce young people to Jesus Christ. I want students to discover their true identity in Jesus. As we look at some of the qualities of Christ I hope to show you how natural, logical, and normal it is for young people to be attracted to him. By painting an accurate picture of the person of Christ to young people, I believe they won't be able to resist him. Instead, they will be stunned by him and will want nothing else than to let go of their fear and pride, and do what he is calling them to do: repent of their sin and surrender to him in love and obedience.

Just as a magnet naturally moves metal, as the compass needle points to the north or south pole, it is inevitable that young will be attracted to Jesus if introduced to him accurately. A normal young person can only resist Jesus if he is misrepresented or if they are extremely dulled by the distractions of the world to the point where they are deaf to his message.

Let me say it again this way: To become a follower of Jesus is not an unusual, or atypical experience. It is completely normal. It's as natural as a flower opening up under the warm rays of the April sun, or for a bird to sing at mating time.

It would be a radical shift for the church if this truth were fully understood: It should be natural, normal, and expected that students become a follower of Jesus before they are eighteen years old.

In many churches people think the norm is that only a few students will come to Christ from time to time. They think that it is normal to only occasionally see youth making a decision to follow Jesus.[1]

I don't believe this at all. I think parents, teachers, pastors, and youth workers should expect young people to want to become loyal followers of Jesus before they reach their twenties! It should be considered a strange, abnormal, almost unexplainable, thing if a boy or girl should grow up (especially in Christian families, churches, and youth groups) and not become a follower of Christ.[2] There is a harvest time in the spiritual realm, and that harvest time is not primarily at the end of the season (i.e. old age), when the grain is matured, or like an ear of corn fully ripe at the end of the season. The spiritual harvest time for people is not when they are ready to pass away, instead it is more toward the other end of life, when they are young. The greatest harvest time seems to be when the eager, energetic young soul is excited to ask the question, "Lord what will you have me to do?" and when she has the courage to respond to Christ's call by saying, "Here I am Lord, send me."

Of course we also long for people to come to Jesus in midlife or the later years. When this happens, it is likely to be noticeable and dramatic, perhaps even astounding.[3] Yet where there is one Apostle Paul (who came to Christ later in life), there are dozens of "Timothys" (who became a disciple of Jesus when he was very young).[4]

If more people began to see early conversion of young people as the normal expected outcome of youth evangelism, then churches would be giving more attention to student ministry.

Yet the perspective of the average adult is that it is normal for all young people to "sow their wild oats." Too many adults believe that the average young person is irresponsible, thoughtless, and not interested in spiritual realities. That could not be further from the truth.

Because of this wrong view, some churches make the terrible mistake of attempting to only entertain young people. Instead, what we need to do is give them the Gospel in a language they can understand. This drills the Good News down to the deepest springs of their being. And when they see Jesus for who he really is, they will naturally want to get to know him and serve him.

Many churches have resorted to just social entertainment as a form of student ministry. Yes, young people often give most of their time to secular activities and sports, yet what they really want is Jesus. They just don't know it yet.[5] I hope this humble book will show how the life of Christ and his teachings appeal especially to young people. I want to demonstrate through the Gospels how when we winsomely present Jesus to young people, the natural, almost inevitable response is to be drawn to him. They will want to accept him as their Pattern and Guide for life. It is truly abnormal and unnatural for young people to reject the Savior of the world when they are given an accurate picture of him. Through this book may some hear Jesus calling: "Come to me."

DISCUSSION QUESTIONS

1. In what ways does Jesus Christ appeal to people in different stages of life?
2. Give some reasons why young people are *especially* attracted to him.
3. Why do you think it is perfectly natural and normal for young people to follow of Jesus?
4. Does this view of the winsome appeal of Jesus do away with the idea of the necessity of conversion? Why not?
5. How did Timothy get introduced to Jesus? Look up the Apostle Paul's statement concerning his mother and grandmother in 2 Timothy 1:5-7; 3:14-17.
6. About what age do you think most people accept Jesus Christ?
7. Why do you think some churches might overly emphasize entertaining young people?

CHAPTER 2

JESUS IS AUTHENTIC

♦ ♦ ♦

A PERSONALITY QUALITY OF JESUS that people don't consider enough is how *authentic* he was. If young people knew how transparent and real Jesus was, I'm guessing they would be incredibly attracted to him. Young people are quick to detect a fake. And they are turned off by a lack of authenticity.

I know a young man who seeks to hide his self-centeredness by a thin veneer of false humility. While always bragging of his own achievements, he constantly tries to cover up his pride by saying, "I have no idea how I've been so lucky."

He has fooled many adults, who say, "What a great guy! He's so humble!" Yet his friends know who he really is. And they mock his self-centeredness.

Youth have a natural ability to smell a fake. And this is another reason why they will be attracted to Jesus if introduced to him accurately. All his words and actions were authentic. Everybody can relate with Jesus' early life. It was just like any other kid.[6] Jesus had a normal childhood too.

Apparently he lived the life of any simple Jewish boy. He learned to study the Bible; he learned how to love his family members, he came under the authority of his parents who were very committed to God. The rabbi in the local school taught him just like everyone else, and when he was old enough, he probably ran errands for his parents and worked in his father's shop.

When he was twelve years old, like every other Jewish boy at that age, he went up with his parents to the Temple in Jerusalem to worship. Like many young people, it seems that he was starting to get a sense of his life mission as a pre-teen. He learned that his mission was to simply serve his Heavenly Father.

His trip to the Temple is the only recorded event of his childhood that even borders on the unusual. After that brief scene in the Temple listening to the most educated teachers of his day, he went right back to his humble home and humble work in Nazareth. And he continued to submit to Joseph and Mary's parental authority for a long time.

Once he left home at about age 30, he started to do many miracles to give testimony to his Divine mission. Think of it this way: If God came to earth, you would expect him to do things that no other human being could do, right? So it is logical to say that each of his miracles was necessary to his mission to demonstrate his Divine nature.

Now let's look at how he chose his first disciples. Interestingly, he simply called them to come follow him. He did not dazzle them, as Napoleon would have done, by winning military battles. He did not promise them unlimited treasures in this world. He didn't guarantee them unlimited sensual delights in the future. He did not mesmerize them with his speaking and logic skills as some philosophers have done. He simply said to a few fishermen, Peter and James and John, "Follow me, and I will make you fishers of men." To Matthew the tax-gatherer, he said, "Come," and to Zacchaeus the tax collector, he declared, "Today I must come over to your house for a visit."

Even though people were drawn to the way Christ spoke with such authority, it was his uncompromising confidence that really attracted them. It was not his looks, the way he dressed, or even the way he used his supernatural power that impressed people.

He did not perform a miracle to persuade any one of his twelve Apostles to follow him. The Apostle Paul was impressed mainly by his teaching, his spirit, and his lifestyle, not because he could raise the dead, or feed the hungry multitudes.

In all of Paul's letters there are few references to Christ's supernatural works. Instead, pages and pages are given to explaining his teachings, and urging followers of Jesus to walk in his steps, and seek "the mind of Christ."

Even his miracles were performed in the most unspectacular and simple ways. He just spoke a simple word and the healing happened, or the loaves were multiplied. In fact, in every possible way he seems to have avoided publicity and notoriety.

For example, he healed the nobleman's son from a distance saying, "Go, your son will live." He asked all of the weeping and wailing mourners (perhaps mourners hired to wail according to the Eastern custom) to leave the room before he said, *"Talitha cumi,"* which means "Daughter, arise." In one of his most notable miracles, the raising of Lazarus from the dead, he simply said, "Lazarus, come forth." And the dead man came forth from the cave where he had been entombed for four days.

After his death and resurrection Jesus was as natural, familiar, and unassuming as he had been before.

On the way to Emmaus even some of his most intimate friends did not recognize him. He walked along with them like any other traveler would have done. And when the disciples saw him on the shore of the lake, he had a simple meal of cooked fish for them. As any considerate friend might do, he invited them to come and have breakfast.

The list of these kinds of illustrations goes on an on. Christ was the most natural, authentic man who ever lived. He was the most "real" man you could ever meet. His Deity did not make him less, but even more human. He did not need anything else to improve his image to others. Everything good and beautiful about humanity was in him already. He just simply shined God's glory because that was his identity—perfectly untainted by sin.

These are just a few examples of why Jesus was so attractive to those who followed him. And still today, young people are drawn to these qualities. So if you want to be an effective leader of young people, begin by becoming preoccupied with these genuine traits of Jesus. Then being shaped by his character you will naturally draw others to him as well.

If you want to become simple, sincere, genuine, and true, like Christ, begin with worshiping him. Be in awe of his life so that you will become like him and your heart will naturally cry out, "Lord I will follow you, wherever you go."

DISCUSSION QUESTIONS

1. Why are young people especially attracted to genuine authenticity in others?

2. In what ways have you seen students show an appreciation for authenticity?

3. Does it seem authentic that Jesus taught the religious leaders in the Temple when he was only twelve years old? If so, why?

4. How did Jesus get his disciples to follow him?

5. How did Jesus display authenticity in the way he performed miracles?

6. List some of his miracles and note some of the details of how he performed them.

7. How do you think an imposter or a self-seeker would have performed miracles?

8. In what ways was Jesus still natural and unassuming after his resurrection?

9. Do you believe that Jesus still today has the same natural, sincere, genuine personality as when he was present on earth?

10. Does Jesus' authenticity appeal to you personally? Why is his "realness" appealing to you?

CHAPTER 3

APPROACHABLE

♦ ♦ ♦

YOUNG PEOPLE TEND TO STAND in awe of great people, and with good reason. It's totally normal for a kid to be nervous about meeting a famous person or someone who is powerful or influential. In fact, it would be arrogant to place yourself on the same level of someone who deserves your respect.

In trying to make friends for the Christian Endeavour movement, I had the opportunity (I share this at the risk of being misunderstood or mocked for saying this) to meet several kings and presidents of republics, and others of equal distinction. I confess that it was somewhat difficult at first to relax, simply because of the ceremony and formalities that go along with people of great influence.

It is not normal to obtain an audience with people like this. You have to make a special appointment through an ambassador, or some important representative on his staff. There are often mountains of red tape that take days or weeks to untangle.[7]

When I would meet dignitaries like this, especially in eastern cultures, I had to bow low. And when I departed I had to back away from his noble presence. You never turn your back upon a king. If it is the Emperor of Japan, for instance, who grants the audience, you must bow three times before coming near him and you must always allow the ruler to lead the conversation. He speaks the first word, and he indicates when the conversation is over.

What a contrast this is to the way men approached Jesus, the King of Kings. No special clothes, no long and tedious formalities, no sitting in the waiting room until it is his pleasure to see you! By contrast, we get the impression from the Gospels that Jesus was completely approachable. He was available and open to interruptions. His disciples sometimes tried to stand between him and the people, but he wouldn't allow it.

When some eager moms brought their children to him, "that his garments might touch them," his disciples rebuked the parents. Then Jesus uttered that classic phrase which has made mothers and children everywhere love him so much: "Let the little children come to me, and do not hinder them, for the Kingdom of Heaven belongs to such as these."

I presume that these parents were poor people, for they did not send their children to Jesus with a nanny. They brought them to Jesus themselves. It's very likely that these children were ragged, snotty-nosed, dirty little specimens of humanity like we might see today in the poor villages of Palestine. But they were not too ragged or dirty for the World's Redeemer to take up in his arms and bless!

Jesus seems to have had dinner with anyone who asked him. Jesus was radically different compared to earthly kings who insulated themselves from the common people. The Heavenly King went wherever he was invited, to the house of Zacchaeus, to Simon's home, to the home of tax gatherers and sinners. Some even accused him of being a "drunk" and a "glutton," because he was so unbiased about whom he would hang out with. He did not try to keep his clothes clean—he was willing to be stained by earthly soil unlike most kings and dignitaries will do. He was not concerned with protecting his image "by the company he kept." His motto seems to have been: "The person who wants to see me is the one I want to see."

Perhaps the best example of his approachability is his conversation with the Samaritan woman. I never fully realized the beauty and the naturalness of this story until when travelling in Samaria I had the opportunity to sit on Jacob's well and imagine hearing the gracious and kind words he used with this woman. With a kind word and a gentle look, Jesus knew how to bridge the tremendous gulf between he and this woman.

He had not come to the well in noble superiority, but as a foot traveler, wearied by his long journey. He sat on the stone wall of the well as if it was his humble throne. Then here comes a woman, from perhaps the neighboring city on the hillside now called Nablous. Think of the contrast! She was a woman; he was a man. This was contrary to all the customs of the day. His hospitality could have been misunderstood as questionable or immoral. It was not okay for a man to talk so freely with an unfamiliar woman. She was a Samaritan. He was a Jew. This was another huge barrier to their conversation. We can barely imagine the great cultural separation between these two. She was a disgraceful woman by the standard of her neighbors. She was living with a man who was not her husband. And yet Jesus, the only absolutely pure man who had ever walked this earth, sits down and wants to befriend this worldly woman.

He did not hesitate to speak first. He started the conversation by asking her for a favor: "Can you please give me a drink?" An earthly king would have *demanded* that she serve him. He would not politely ask for a favor like Jesus did. Then the conversation carried on naturally. It was if two equals were talking together. Read the story again to the very last word, and you will notice how Jesus led her so naturally to open up and share her life story. Then he surprised her in response to her vulnerability: "I, the one speaking to you—I am he...." The Messiah, the Christ, the Desire of all nations, the One whom prophets foretold, of whom the Psalmist sang, is here in your midst!

We see in so many other instances how Jesus made it easy for people to approach him. He was never cold, prideful, or cynical. He never displayed an attitude that would paralyze even the most timid of people from enjoying free and open conversation with him. He made people who needed him comfortable and relaxed so they would open up.

Young people need to hear about Jesus' approachability. From a young person's perspective, he is the perfect person to have as a close friend. Remember, he is not any different today. He is the same yesterday, today and forever. Give him a chance and see for yourself. If you can say nothing else about him, at least say, "I do believe; help me overcome my unbelief!" And, just like that guy who came up to him so many centuries ago with those words, you too can receive your heart's desire by seeking to know Jesus. You will begin to understand for yourself that he is nearer to you than you can imagine. He is always easy to approach. Like when he healed the afflicted son of the believing father, or when he talked with the woman who had many husbands, at the well in Samaria, Jesus is approachable to you too.

Discussion Questions

1. Why is it a good idea to respect those in high position?
2. How might you feel if you met a king or president for the first time?
3. Did Jesus Christ demand that people salute him or show reverence toward him like people in high position do today?
4. Even though he was far greater than the greatest of men, why did people find it so easy to approach Jesus?
5. Give some examples of his approachability.
6. What are some examples of when children, young people, and very poor people came to him?
7. Did he reject "bad" people? Look for three Scriptural examples of his interactions with people like this.
8. Did he ever ride into Jerusalem as a king? When was that? Share some of the details of that story. What does this show you about his approachability?
9. How did he treat women? What was remarkable about his treatment of them?
10. How do these examples give us confidence when we approach him now?
11. How can we approach him today? How does it personally make you feel that he is so approachable? What are some practical ways you can approach Jesus in your prayer and devotions?

CHAPTER 4
HUMBLE

◆ ◆ ◆

HUMILITY IS A PERSONALITY TRAIT that is closely related to authenticity. A prideful person is never humble. He is always thinking of himself, always posing, always saying to himself, "What will others think of me?" The hearts of all people (but especially of the young) are instinctively drawn to people who are unassuming. We desire to spend time with humble people because they don't place themselves above us. They don't think more highly of themselves than they should.

Any other mere man would have been tempted to use the supernatural powers Jesus had to show off or impress people.

In fact, that was one of the ways Satan tried to tempt Jesus in the wilderness. The devil taunted him to jump from the high point of the Temple and let his angels catch him. The crowds would have loved to see someone leap from a building and come out unscathed! He would have been the talk of the town. He would be set on a pedestal of popularity higher than the Temple itself. But Jesus never performed a miracle for his own glory or to attract attention to himself.

Over and over again Jesus must have been tempted with such power, but every time he was able to say, "Get behind me, Satan."

He was truly humble in the way he lived. Yet humility is not only shown in words, is it? Pride also rears its ugly head in our actions. Extravagance is one form of pride. People often live beyond their means for the sake of amassing wealth. Or a woman might dress to the nines for the sake of getting noticed. This is all motivated by pride.

Jesus had all of the gold and silver of the world at his disposal, and the cattle upon a thousand hills. Yet instead of taking control of all that was his, he chose to live in poverty. His famous phrase has become a classic in all languages: "Foxes have holes, and the birds of the air have nests; but the Son of man has nowhere to lay his head."

Poverty in itself is neither humble nor prideful. One who brags and boasts might actually be hiding the fact that they have nothing to their name. And a wealthy person, for the sake of humanity, can live humbly by choosing to live the life of a servant.

Yet no one has dared to call Jesus a prideful boaster. This is really strange because he boldly claimed to be the Son of God. He dared to say, "I and my Father are one." He declared to all mankind, "I am the Way, the Truth and the Life", and "No man comes to the Father but by me!" In these statements it would seem that he has opened himself up for criticism. Don't these sound like prideful statements? Yet you cannot find a single person who will dare to accuse Jesus of being prideful.

We will look at more examples of why Jesus has always been respected for his modesty, humility, and self-denial. But the fact remains that Jesus made profound boasts about his relationship with the Father. And yet he maintained a life of absolute humility of speech and action. This should be enough to convince any person of his Deity. Only Jesus could pull this off.

As the saying goes: "A person is known by the company they keep?" Yet Jesus usually hung out with people of low socio-economic status. Given his Divinity, one might have expected him to be the guest of princes and kings. Pilate would have loved to entertain such a miracle-worker if it hadn't have caused a riot among the religious leaders. But instead, Christ preferred fishermen and tax-gatherers. He did not hesitate to turn away the rich young ruler who could not accept his standard of self-sacrifice.

He preferred the friends he made, not because they were poor and underprivileged, but because they were "meek and lowly in *heart...*" in other words, they were humble and unassuming, not self-important and self-sufficient.

And then think of that radical moment when he dressed himself with a servant's towel and washed his disciples' feet! He did this to give us a living example of humility. He was willing to submit to the most menial service toward others, and he did not consider this action disgraceful or undignified.

This kind of modesty and humility, coupled with courage and dignity are the kinds of qualities that appeal to every normal young person. When they see this man who never lowered his standard or denied his fate to suffer for mankind, they are drawn to him. As I have said before, young people resent people who are fake, and Jesus in all of these examples proves himself time and again that he was anything but a fraud.

Once on the street a young man said to me, "I don't like that pastor. I won't go to his church because he seems so stuck on himself." Of course he may have misjudged that pastor, but his words show the natural resentment young people have toward religious goody-goodys who can't stoop down to other people's level.

When scrutinizing the person of Jesus Christ, the Shepherd of Shepherds, young people will never find even the slightest bit of prideful superiority in him. Instead of pointing the finger at people, his sermons were parables. He drove the truth home with a familiar story that appealed to the most simple of minds.

Though he is Lord of all, he was also a "friend of tax collectors and sinners." However young, insignificant, and unnoticed you might feel, you are not unnoticed by Jesus. If you respond to him with humility and submit to him fully, you too will start to become like him. Following this man sounds adventurous, doesn't it? Count me in!

DISCUSSION QUESTIONS

1. What do you think are some qualities of true humility?
2. Do young people generally admire a humble person?
3. How do they show their respect for humble people?
4. In what ways did Jesus show humility in his character?
5. Mention some examples that illustrate his humility.
6. How do we reconcile his humility with his statements that might sound prideful like, "I and the Father are one"?
7. Did his enemies accuse him of pride or egotism? Mention the one example of this mentioned in this chapter. Why do skeptics not accuse him of this today?
8. Is there any difference between being reserved and being humble? If so, what is it? In what ways was Jesus both humble and reserved? Why do you think they are both consistent with courage and dignity?
9. Why do you think young people in particular would be attracted to Jesus' humility?
10. How might we too work on developing humility in our lives?

CHAPTER 5

COURAGEOUS

♦ ♦ ♦

THERE ARE TWO KINDS OF courage: moral and physical. Jesus Christ had both. He was physically daring. He was morally brave. The Disciples loved this about Jesus. And young people today are attracted to these qualities in him. No young person wants to follow a coward.

It baffles me why some people still present Jesus as the "meek and mild," the "humble Nazarene," the "Preacher of non-resistance" who allowed himself to be captured, tried, condemned and crucified without a struggle. We make him out to be a passivist because he wouldn't allow his Disciples to fight when the mob arrested him in the Garden of Gethsemane. I fear that if we present Jesus in this light to young people they will get the wrong idea about him.

In contrast to the type of courage that Jesus displayed, the "courage" of a bully is really just tyranny over the weak. A bully is usually a coward when he meets his match. There are other forms of worldly "courage" that don't really describe Jesus either. For example, the courage of a boxer or a prizefighter is merely callousness mixed with a desire for fame and the cash prize.

By contrast, real courage is the willingness to suffer for a great cause. This kind of courage is just as possible for the most gentle of girls as it is for the armored warrior. If this is true, then Jesus Christ is the supreme example of physical and moral courage. The world has never seen a more courageous person.

Let me prove this by the evidence of Scripture. On one occasion, Jesus discovered that the moneychangers and sales-men had polluted the Temple with their selfish ambitions. It had actually become the norm to profane the Temple with self-centered, commercial transactions. Of course the people and the religious leaders justified it because they thought it was necessary to sell doves and lambs for sacrifices in the Temple. They "needed to provide these services for the masses." So they exchanged the people's Roman currency for the coins of the Temple treasury.

But Christ saw right through this. To him, Temple wor-ship was becoming commercialized. Merchants were there for what they could get out of it. They weren't selling sacrificial animals and grain for the convenience of the worshippers. They were making his Father's house a den of thieves. Now check out what Jesus did about it. He confronted this hypoc-risy completely on his own. He was unprotected and unarmed. The business people and the Temple worshippers were all against him.

But as usual, Jesus' courage was up to the challenge. He was one man against the multitude with a whip of cords, a symbol of punishment and cleansing. He could have chosen a more effective instrument to turn the market upside down. Yet he drove them all out, and cleansed the place, with one majestic burst of righteous indignation. It was not the strand of small cords that did it; it was his moral and physical courage that made the selfish peddlers flee. There was never a more magnificent expression of true bravery.

This wasn't the only time Jesus did something like this. How about the event that took place at the very end of his life. He had been betrayed and he knew it. The soldiers came to arrest him in the Garden of Gethsemane. His disciples were inspired for the moment with their master's courage. They were ready to fight. Peter even drew his sword to defend Jesus. The only chance of escape was fight or flight. A coward would have taken the chance to run. Yet Jesus even knowing that he would be condemned and executed if he was arrested did not run. He was brave enough to surrender his only opportunity to flee, and said to Peter, "Put away your sword!"

I think there is nothing more awe-inspiring in all of blood-stained world history than the arrest of Jesus in the Garden. John writes, "Jesus, knowing all that was going to happen to him, went out and asked them, 'Who is it you want?' 'Jesus of Nazareth,' they replied. 'I am he,' Jesus said. (And Judas the traitor was standing there with them.) When Jesus said, 'I am he,' they drew back and fell to the ground." (see John 18:5-6)

Being willing to sacrifice yourself for the needs of others is always a sign of courage. Yet Jesus demonstrated extreme generosity and courage like no one had ever seen before. The soldiers were astonished at his simple declaration and godlike appearance. They "drew back and fell to the ground." The soldiers were the cowards. Christ was the hero. He even had to ask them again, "Who is it you want?" And again he had to say, "I told you that I am he. If you are looking for me, then let these men go."

Oh young people! Have you ever heard of such absolute, unflinching courage, mixed with tender unselfishness before? For a mere man who could not see how this was going to turn out, surrendering to such injustice like this is almost unthinkable. Jesus knew all of the things that were about to happen to him: the beatings, the whipping, the spitting, the purple robe, the cross, the thirst, the agony of death, and yet he calmly said: "I told you that I am he... let these men go."

And his supreme courage never waned. He did not call for legions of angels who would have defended him. He did not pray that the cup of agony might pass from him, unless it was the Father's will. Then he confronted Pilate with undaunted courage. Pilate was even irritated by Jesus' calm refusal to plead his case or defend himself. He said to Jesus, "Don't you realize I have power either to free you or to crucify you?" Jesus answered, 'You would have no power over me if it were not given to you from above." (see John 19:11)

Calm, dignified, and courageous to the very end, no soldiers could terrify him. No ruler could intimidate him. No adverse circumstances could shake his courage. No slings and arrows of injustice could unnerve him. I could tell even more examples from the Gospels that would prove the courage of

Jesus Christ, but I will settle for just a few extremely courageous statements that he regularly repeated throughout his life.

Jesus often asserted that he was the Son of God, and the Savior of mankind. He called himself the Way, the Truth, and the Life. He referred to himself as the Good Shepherd, the Door into the Sheep pen. He declared that he and the Father were one: that no one could come to the Father except through him. He knew his goals were supreme, and that only *he* could accomplish them.

How does this prove his courage? Well, consider what the people thought of him at the time. He was a peasant's son, a carpenter by trade, and a poor, simple man from a humble family. Even Napoleon would not have had the courage to make such claims that he was the Son of God. Julius Caesar and Alexander the Great, although allowing themselves to be worshipped as gods, would have shrunk from making the demand of universal worship and headship that Jesus made.

These are either the claims of the world's most colossal narcissist, the crazy declarations of a lunatic, or they are the true demands of the most courageous person the world has ever seen. The Christian world has always rejected the first two of these hypotheses: and these past nineteen centuries of Christianity disprove them as well. Every intelligent young person is repulsed by the idea that Jesus was "full of himself." That can't be true. The last possibility (that he was the most courageous person the world has ever seen) is the only hypothesis that has stood the test of time. Jesus Christ is the supreme human example of Godlike courage. He was who he claimed to be. He dared to make that claim. He *is* the Son of God. It's undeniable.

DISCUSSION QUESTIONS

1. What misconceptions of Jesus do you think people have today? Why do so many people still believe these misconceptions?
2. How would you define true courage in your own words?
3. In what ways did Jesus display true courage?
4. Do you think it requires courage at times *not* to fight? When did Jesus demonstrate courage like that?
5. Does it require courage to be just, kind and generous? Describe some ways Jesus exemplified true courage mixed with gentleness?
6. Was it cowardly for Jesus to ask the Father to consider allowing the cup of crucifixion to pass from him? Why or why not? What are some things you learn from that conversation Jesus had with his Father.
7. Why did it require supreme courage for Jesus to claim to be the Divine Son of God in his culture? What would you think of someone today who would make such a claim?
8. Why were the Jews held accountable for rejecting Christ's claims? If we reject him, are we not also accountable to God for that?
9. If we reject him, what dilemma does that put us in regarding our relationship with the Heavenly Father?

CHAPTER 6

CONSIDERATE

♦ ♦ ♦

IF THERE WERE ONE QUALITY in a friend that you would say is essential, what would it be? A friend may be authentic, honest, brave, witty and wise, but if he lacks a genuine heart of love, or is inconsiderate of our feelings, it will be hard to connect with him at the deepest level wouldn't it? If a person is not considerate or respectful toward us, we may admire him, respect him, honor him, and even think highly of him, but we won't want him for a friend.

I know of some really noble people, yet it makes me cringe when they ring the doorbell. You could not pay me to go on a long vacation with them. Someone has defined a best friend as one whom you would prefer above all others to have with you if you were shipwrecked on a desert island.

Surely such a definition is more than applicable to Christ, the Friend of Friends. Many Christians have been happy in a lonely prison cell because his great Friend, Jesus was with him.

I think young people are especially aware of this quality in others, though they may not really think about it. They instinctively avoid people who have no heart for others, no matter how brilliant or put together they might be. I know a very godly and capable evangelist who is very ineffective with young people because he is harsh, rigid and inconsiderate of their feelings.

But Jesus is so different than this! He is truly loving and considerate. Mary and Martha welcomed him in their house because they knew he loved them. He had a deep loving heart for people. The Bible even records the detail that Jesus wept at his friend Lazarus' grave. The Jews saw this and remarked, "See how he loved him!" Apparently, his human affection was something astonishing. His love for others stood out in contrast to other religious leaders. He shed genuine tears of human affection at that open grave that day.

But real affection is not always best demonstrated in words or by a dramatic show of emotions. Just because someone sheds tears for the death of a loved one does not prove their love for him. Placing flowers on the casket isn't the proof of one's love. Instead, it is the kind, considerate acts they consistently displayed toward the person while they were alive that truly demonstrates their love. Jesus was the supreme example of this kind of love. To understand this we must remember who he was and who his friends were. Jesus was an uncrowned king among people who rarely understood him. He was a God-man among violent, cowardly men. He was a leader among bad-mannered followers who were slow to understand. Yet he seldom corrected them. Instead, he had astonishing patience for them!

Even when Peter dared to disagree with him, Jesus did not resent him for that. Peter refused to allow Jesus to wash his feet and impulsively said, "You shall never wash my feet." But Jesus saw the real love and respect that provoked Peter's passion, and instead of saying, "I have no time for your temper tantrums, I will have John do it," he quietly said, "Then you have no part with me." Through Jesus' patient response, Peter immediately saw the deep significance of this act of service. (see John 13)

If Jesus had been merely a man, Peter's personality would have provoked him to anger so many times. Even when Peter denied Jesus three times Jesus did not reply bitterly, but instead looked sadly upon his betrayal: "And the Lord turned and looked at Peter." (see Luke 22:61)

The other disciples would have tested him to the point of anger as well, had he not loved them like a mother loves her child. When Philip said, "Show us the Father, and that will be enough," there seems to have been a note of deep disappointment mixed with tender love when Jesus replied, "Don't you know me, Philip, even after I have been among you such a long time?" (see John 14:8-9)

When Thomas, the skeptic, continued to doubt Jesus, even though there was so much evidence of Jesus' resurrection, (evidence that had apparently convinced *all* of the other Disciples) he did not turn Thomas away with a rebuke for his ridiculous, self-righteous skepticism, but simply said, "Put your finger here; see my hands. Reach out your hand and put it into my side. Stop doubting and believe." (see John 20:27)

When the Disciples fell asleep in Gethsemane, his only rebuke was the gentle words, "Couldn't you men keep watch with me for one hour?" And when they fell asleep again, while Jesus was going through agony worse than death, he did not even show disappointment in their insensitivity. Considerate of their tired bodies and heavy eyes, he only said, "Are you still sleeping and resting?" (see Matthew 26:36-46)

Looking at other accounts where Jesus displayed respect and care for others, we see his love for the multitude in the way he miraculously supplied food for them when they were hungry and a long way from towns where bread and fish could be purchased. He showed sensitivity for his tired disciples when he invited them to come withdraw from the busyness of ministry among the crowds to get some needed rest: "For he knows how we are formed, he remembers that we are dust."[8]

A general in the army would not put up with anxiety, rudeness and ignorance among his soldiers. No king would put up with his servants behaving like this. Yet in contrast, the King of Kings put up with all of these kinds of behaviors because he loved people so deeply.

Jesus provides a great example for young people because even when he was young, living under the authority of his parents, he was considerate to his parents while living in Nazareth. He evidently had some foreshadows of his Divinity, though he may not have fully realized it, yet this apparently never caused him to place himself above his peasant parents. For example, imagine the Son of God drawing water at the neighborhood well. The Son of God picking up sticks for his mom to cook on the fire. The Son of God planing wood, and shaping the yokes and goads for the oxen in his dad's workshop, and doing it without a sign of condescending superiority.

Yes, from boyhood to manhood, all of the way to the cross, he showed his love by being extremely considerate toward others. Young men and women, I encourage you to study the story of Jesus when he was a boy in Nazareth, until your hearts, begin to beat with love for others, and your lives demonstrate Jesus' love through considerate acts of kindness.

I do not believe, as some think, that young people are attracted only by boldness and overconfidence.[9] I know that young people do not always show thoughtfulness to others, but I do believe they appreciate when they see people show love and gentleness toward others. Young people respect those that display quiet self-sacrifice. They admire the love that is long suffering, the love that does not envy, and the love that does not brag, or pat itself on the back. They respect those who are patient in all things, believe in others, and they admire those who hope confidently in God. This is the kind of love that never fails. The Apostle Paul must have been looking in his Master's wounded face when he wrote those words: "In your relationships with one another, have the same mindset as Christ Jesus." (Philippians 2:5)

DISCUSSION QUESTIONS

1. What are some character traits that help you develop close friendships with others?
2. In what difficult circumstances did Jesus prove his friendship toward others?
3. Mention the names of some of Jesus' closest friends you read about in the Bible.
4. Share some of the personality traits of Mary, Martha, Peter, and Thomas.
5. What was perhaps one of the greatest trials that Jesus had to endure in his life on earth?
6. How did Jesus show his love for the average person in his daily life?
7. Share some of the details of the story of the loaves and fishes and of his childhood in Nazareth. In what ways did Jesus show that he was considerate toward others in these situations?
8. In what ways did Jesus show his incredible patience and considerateness toward people who were walking in sin?
9. In what ways can courage also be shown through gentleness?
10. What is a practical step you could take to grow in being considerate toward others like Jesus was?

CHAPTER 7

CAREFREE

◆ ◆ ◆

SOME PEOPLE FEEL LIKE THEY must preserve the traditions of the past. Traditions do have their place. They provide a living link between the old days and the present. They conserve some things that are good. But the danger with traditions is that they might cause us to hold on to some things that are outdated and irrelevant. People with a bent toward holding on to traditions are naturally cautious, and resist unwise pendulum swings toward innovations that might have long term negative consequences.[10]

Yet there is one problem with folks like this. Young people are not likely to follow people who are overly-cautious or legalistic. People who have lost touch with the natural, spontaneous, genuine, human element in life will not attract kids. Legalists are overly concerned with what others do and think. They are preoccupied with right and wrong rather than relationships.

The Pharisees who lived during Christ's days were extreme examples of these types of people. Almost everything they did was done because somebody else had done the same thing before them. They were bound by rules, order, and traditions. In the original Greek there is a touch of humor in Mark's description of one of their habits, "(The Pharisees and all the Jews do not eat unless they give their hands a ceremonial washing, holding to the tradition of the elders. When they come from the marketplace they do not eat unless they wash. And they observe many other traditions, such as the washing of cups, pitchers and kettles.)" (see Mark 7:3)

When Mark speaks of the Jews washing their hands all of the time, the word he uses is, "ceremonially," or perhaps it means, "up to the elbow." In other words, *they washed their hands thoroughly whether they were dirty or not.* This seems funny doesn't it? Why wash your hands when they aren't dirty? And the Pharisees didn't stop there. They washed their dishes and utensils whether they needed to be washed or not. But ironically, they were not so diligent in maintaining purity in their moral behavior. They neglected their own parents and refused to provide for them, claiming that their property belonged to God and therefore they could not give it away. Jesus recognized this hypocritical traditionalism had become so deeply engrained that it needed to be confronted directly. There is no more scathing rebuke of this rampant traditionalism, than is found in this seventh chapter of Mark, "Therefore you nullify the word of God by your tradition that you have handed down. And you do many things like that." (Mark 7:13)

Jesus came to free people from this kind of slavery to the Law. Religion is the ultimate enemy of grace. Jesus knew there was no life in merely following rules. When people try to please God through religious practices rather than through an intimate relationship with Christ, they miss out on the abundant life. They quench the Spirit who wants them to be free. "Don't you see that whatever enters the mouth goes into the stomach and then out of the body? But the things that come out of a person's mouth come from the heart, and these defile them." (Matthew 15:17-18) Instead of washing pots and pans and scrubbing your hands and arms all the way up to your elbows, Jesus placed importance on confession and repentance so that one's heart could be cleansed from evil thoughts, adultery, fornication, murder, theft, jealousy, wickedness, lying, blasphemy, pride, and foolishness.

It is difficult for us today to realize how much the religious elite had put pressure and guilt on people to follow their traditions and rules. Some of their restrictions were so immature and ridiculous that we can't read them without cracking up. Not only was eating eggs that had been laid on the Sabbath forbidden, but eating eggs laid on the day after the Sabbath was also taboo because the hen had been working to prepare the egg within their body on the Sabbath Day!

These rules seem ridiculous to us. So it is not difficult to see why Jesus Christ was so annoyed by them. He broke out of the norm and radically tore down the bonds of tradition. He shattered the artificial barriers that religion had put up. He removed the blockades, which kept people from enjoying God and freely worshipping him without guilt or obligation.

The way Jesus conducted his ministry seems refreshing to us, yet you have to realize that what Jesus taught and even *how* he taught completely broke the molds of tradition back then. For example: The Pharisees thought it was proper to preach in the synagogue whereas Jesus often preached in open fields. Jesus taught from the platform of a rocking boat on the edge of a lake. The Pharisees occupied their time by splitting theological hairs over insignificant questions about the law. They wrote bulky commentaries on questions that were irrelevant to most people. In contrast, Jesus taught with stories, illustrations and parables. He taught people about God's care for his children by pointing out that God even cares for a sparrow falling to the ground. How much more does he care for us! He told them about God's love of beauty by pointing to the flowers in a field. He taught about how God forgives people by telling a story of a rebellious boy who wandered off into a foreign land and finally came crawling back to his father when he came to his senses. He explained how God searches for his lost children by telling a story of a poor woman looking for a small coin that rolled off of her table onto the floor of her hut. Then he reemphasized this point by telling a story of a shepherd who searched for one lonely sheep that was lost on a dark mountainside.

As far as I know, Christ never preached a sermon that the Pharisees would have thought was worth listening to. Talking among themselves they must have said, "He is just a dreamer and a story-teller. Why should we pay attention to a man who talks about seeds and birds and farmers and fishermen's nets and the clouds in the sky, and has nothing to say about Hillel and the great teachers of the law?"

Not only was Jesus radical in his teaching, but his *lifestyle* was extreme as well. The Pharisees had taken away the enjoyment of the Sabbath Day so much that it was impossible to even do anything merciful towards people in need. People didn't even have the freedom to perform the necessary duties of every-day life on the Sabbath. They were like mummies who had wrapped themselves in their own cloths until they couldn't even move their hands and feet on the day that should have been the most enjoyable day of the week! Jesus knew that it was going to take something radical to break the snares that trapped people, to free their souls.

We know from the historical record of Jesus that he accomplished just that. Not by arguing with the Pharisees, or by condemning the traditions of the elders, but simply by using common sense. He told them that it was *right* to do good on the Sabbath Day. The Pharisees would have left the man with the withered hand helpless forever rather than heal him on the Sabbath Day. (see Luke 5) Yet Jesus said to him, "Stretch out your hand." He restored it completely like his other hand, and in doing so, he taught the world that it is right to do good and save a life, even on your day off. Duh!

While the disciples were walking through a wheat field, they plucked some of the ears of grain and rubbed them in their hands to have a bite to eat. Giving permission to his disciples to do this on the Sabbath completely shocked the religious leaders of the day. They interpreted this action as a rebellious disregard for the Law of Moses. They thought Jesus and his disciples were doing something almost worthy of death. But again Christ tore open these man-made shackles. These stupid laws weren't God's ideas. They had made this stuff up. This was never the intent of Moses' law. Jesus said, "The Sabbath was made for man, not man for the Sabbath." (Mark 2:27)

We have to understand that even though Jesus' actions seemed like a radical change because he completely ignored the traditions of the Pharisees, in actuality he never set aside any real laws of God. He never condoned any disregard for God's commands that were meant to cause reverence and worship in the hearts of people. He very clearly tells us that he came not to destroy the Law but to fulfill it. He simply freed the mummies who were all bound up in man-made rules. He simply tore the cords and freed the religiously oppressed so that the people could once again embrace the real purposes of God.

I believe if young people today could learn about the life of Christ from this angle, understanding the context of the life and times that Jesus lived, they would see just how radical he really was. He confronted narrow-minded traditions, and exposed the prejudices that even his disciples struggled with. By looking at how Jesus dismantled such monumental religious hypocrisy, one must conclude that only a mastermind could have done this. Only God in the flesh could have stood against such numbing traditions and religious regulations and have won that cultural battle like Jesus did.

In the Chamber of Horrors at Nuremburg is a terrible image called the "Iron Maiden." It is hollow in the middle and studded with sharp iron spikes on the inside. People who had to endure the ultimate torture of the Inquisition were placed within the iron maiden, and very, very gradually the doors through which the person entered closed on him. Perhaps at times it took hours to clamp it down upon the unfortunate victim. Little by little the spikes tore into his tender flesh until they met. This crushed the person to death.

It was an "Iron Maiden" of tradition and regulation in which the Pharisees were intellectually trapped. Their life of faith was being crushed out. The very spirit of God in the hearts of men was impaled on these cruel spikes of tradition, until Christ came and opened the doors. He liberated the spirit of people by his grace, and the possibility of an intimate relationship with God was once again restored. Jesus freed God's people from their prison of traditions and Laws.

DISCUSSION QUESTIONS

1. What positive things can you see in people who hold staunchly to tradition? Yet why are we not usually comfortable being around people like this for very long?

2. Who were the religious elite people who held so firmly to traditions and laws during the time of Jesus? In what ways did they demonstrate their legalism?

3. How did Jesus rebuke their overbearing traditionalism? Talk about some of the examples of his rebukes mentioned in this chapter and see if you can relate to how Jesus felt about such legalism?

4. Why does he rebuke them for their over-concern with people having perfect behavior?

5. What better things did Jesus want for people that the Pharisees' traditions were keeping them from enjoying?

6. What were some of the alternative teaching styles that Jesus used to instruct people that were different than the Pharisees?

7. Did Jesus really teach that people didn't need to be reverent about observing the Sabbath?

8. What distinction did he make about the Sabbath when he healed the withered arm? (see Luke 5:17-26)

9. How do you think Jesus would want us to enjoy the Sabbath Day today?

CHAPTER 8

FUNNY

♦ ♦ ♦

YOUNG PEOPLE APPRECIATE A GOOD sense of humor. Another word for funny is "witty," and witty people know how to say the right thing at the right time. So many of us are clumsy with our words and don't know how to take advantage of good timing. One thing that young people love about Jesus is that here is a guy who never seemed to be at a loss of words. He always had a way of saying the right thing at the right time. And sometimes he was really funny.

I do not use the word "wit" in the sense that you would describe a jokester. And I don't even use it to describe someone who has a knack for entertaining. Jesus was witty because he was a master of knowledge. A witty person knows how to turn a conversation toward something familiar to everyone in order to make a point or change the mood at just the right moment.

One danger that witty people have to watch out for is that they can become critical or cut people down. The witty person is sometimes so eager to get a rise out of people that he will say something that might hurt others just to get a laugh. Jesus never did this. He used his wit to speak truth, often times to make a serious point, or to express his love for people by poking fun at something everyone struggled with. Yet even when responding to his critics, Jesus was courteous when he probably could have made them look like a fool.

Obviously young people will not respect or want to entrust themselves to someone who uses their wit to cut others down.

Let's look at four examples of Jesus' wittiness to show how his response to people often left them speechless. These examples show how he masterfully commanded his intellect, knowledge, and life experience, with great awareness of his audience and the timing of the moment.

At one time the Disciples came to him with a classic, selfish question that so often seemed to trouble them: "Who is greatest in the Kingdom of Heaven?" We don't know if this was a purely academic question that related to their concerns about different levels of leadership, or whether they wanted him to decide who should have the authority in their group between Peter, James, John and the others.

How would you have answered this question? If it was me I might have said, "Wow, really? Seriously? That's a really dumb question." Yet an answer like this would not have been very effective and it would have missed the opportunity to speak seriously about a flaw in their understanding of the ways of Christ's Kingdom.

Instead of responding this way, Jesus saw an opportunity. Seeing a little child playing nearby, he said, "Come here, little guy." I imagine he called him with a gentle voice and a kind smile because the little child didn't hesitate to run to him. He stood there in the midst of a strange group of men, and Jesus said to the group: "Therefore, whoever takes the lowly position of this child is the greatest in the Kingdom of Heaven."

I think this child must have been very young, just beginning to walk, perhaps. Young children seem to have a no fear, a limited self-will, and they don't struggle with any of the shy self-consciousness that older children show. According to Jesus this child was the greatest of all of them because he was the most humble, and he probably didn't have a prideful estimation of himself yet.

As you can see, Jesus' was aware of the issue at hand and had the wit to speak into it. He taught the whole group a valuable lesson: "For all those who exalt themselves will be humbled, and those who humble themselves will be exalted." Jesus' witty style seemed to enable him to say everything that needed to be said without leaving behind too much of a sting or bad aftertaste.

Three other examples of this kind of wit are found in Matthew 22. Before his crucifixion the Jews seemed to constantly try to catch Jesus in his words, thinking that maybe if they could just discredit him in the eyes of the people, then they wouldn't have to resort to more controversial and harsher methods to shut him up. The last thirty verses of Matthew 22 are perfect examples of the keen, sharp, and kind-hearted wit that Jesus used to confront people in their sin.

The first question the Pharisees used to try to trap Jesus was the classic burning question of their day: "Is it lawful to pay taxes to Caesar?" For the average person, this was a brilliant trap. If he said, "Yes," the Jews would hate him and he would lose his influence with his own people. If he said, "No," the Romans would presume that he was a troublemaker.

So what did he do? He neither said "Yes" or "No", but asked someone to bring him a denarius (a silver coin worth about $4.00.)[11] As he examined the Emperor's face and inscription on the coin he said, "Whose image and name is this?" They replied, "Caesar's." In that word they answered their own question themselves. They were already paying tribute to Caesar through their taxes. They were using his coins. They were under his government therefore they were acknowledging his sovereignty. Humoring them, he answered their question but got to the heart of the issue. Jesus essentially showed them how trivial it was to argue about taxes, which were merely an indicator of the governmental authority they were under. But their supreme authority was God. God was actually sovereign over their whole lives. "So give back to Caesar what is Caesar's, and to God what is God's." How ironic that these Pharisees were distracted by politics and complained about the oppression of the Roman government, yet hadn't the slightest concern for the weight of religiosity they were putting on the people's shoulders! What a double standard.

Next the Sadducees took their turn and asked a really foolish question about the widow who had been married a few times. These guys didn't believe in any resurrection at all, so they thought they had him trapped for sure.

But no matter how smart they thought they were, Jesus just cut through their arrogance and said: "You are in error because you do not know the Scriptures or the power of God. At the resurrection people will neither marry nor be given in marriage; they will be like the angels in heaven." Then Jesus quoted Exodus 3 to silence the Sadducees further. He knew that they did not believe in life after death, so he quoted their own Scriptures to disprove them. In this passage, God says to Moses: "I *am* the God of Abraham, Isaac and Jacob." Then Jesus said, "He is not the God of the dead but of the living." The implication of his statement (which they would not have missed as Old Testament scholars) was that Abraham, Isaac and Jacob *are* now living; therefore there *is* a resurrection. Jesus' wit silenced the Sadducees. They apparently had nothing else to say.

Then the Pharisees took their turn and tried one more time to trap Jesus. A prominent and skilled lawyer on their side asked Jesus, "Teacher, which is the greatest commandment in the Law?" We don't know exactly how they expected to catch him with this question, but it is quite possible that they thought they could confuse him since there were so many laws to choose from. There were ceremonial laws, foods that were prohibited, etc. Which law would Jesus put above all of the others? "Surely," they thought, "He won't have a good answer for this question."

And once again, they were wrong. Christ blew them away with his response: "Love the Lord your God with all your heart and with all your soul and with all your mind and with all your strength.' The second is this: 'Love your neighbor as yourself.' There is no commandment greater than these."

These are just a few examples that show the wittiness of Jesus. In the spur of the moment, Jesus said things off the cuff that had such substance, that they were never forgotten. No wonder people said about him: "No one could say a word in reply, and from that day on no one dared to ask him any more questions."

This is the One whom I want to invite young people to follow. He was no intellectual push over. Jesus was the most amazing human example of wittiness that the world has ever known. He wasn't tripped up by fine sounding arguments. He didn't miss a beat and jumped at the opportunity to take up any challenge or mockery people could throw at him. Yet he was so gentle and compassionate that he could rebuke pride and selfishness by simply pointing to a little child as a living parable.

All of Jesus' responses to people inspire confidence in him. There is no one more worthy to follow. There is no one safer whom you could ever submit your life to.

DISCUSSION QUESTIONS

1. How would you define wittiness in the way we've described it in this chapter?
2. In what ways was Jesus' response witty when he spoke to the Disciples about who would be greatest?
3. What are some of the reasons why you think the Jews wanted to trap Jesus in his words?
4. What trap did the religious leaders set for him regarding the taxes the Jews had to pay to Rome? In what ways would have a "Yes" or "No" answer discredited him? Instead, how did he answer them? What are some things you think his response accomplished?
5. What did the Sadducees not believe in? Recount the story of the trap the Sadducees set for Jesus in Matthew 22:23-33. How did he answer them?
6. How did he prove the reality of life after death from the Scriptures?
7. What does Jesus wittiness teach us about him?

CHAPTER 9

ENTHUSIASTIC

◆ ◆ ◆

MOST OF US LIKE TO be around people who are generally in a good mood. An unhappy whiner is probably not going to have much success in building relationships with young people. The enthusiastic cheerfulness of Jesus is probably one of his most notable personality qualities. This is another reason why young people are so attracted to him.

Some people only imagine Jesus as serious. They wonder whether Jesus ever really smiled or not. Of course he smiled, and probably belly-laughed too! If he didn't, then how else could he have had such a following?

Children would not have run to a miserable man who was too serious. Yet they ran to Jesus. The dismal face that never relaxes from worry does not win people, but Jesus won all sorts of people with his winsome personality.

You might think that Jesus was so oppressed with the sins and sorrows of mankind that he could not have smiled or laughed. But we must also remember the perspective that he had of the Father and of the paradise that awaited those who would follow him. He knew personally what the Father's love was like, and he knew what it was like to be in the Father's presence. He was also convinced of the final victory of good over evil. Therefore he had more reasons for being cheerful and enthusiastic than any other human that has lived on earth.

So how do we know he was so cheerful and enthusiastic? Fortunately we are not left to speculate on this aspect of his personality. His own words give proof of his enthusiasm. In fact, he often spoke of having "good cheer."

Let's consider some of the events in the Bible where Jesus' cheerfulness is highlighted. Once a paralyzed man, lying on a mattress, was brought to Christ by his friends. When Jesus met the man, guess what he said first? You might expect him to first address his paralysis by telling him to "get up and walk, you are healed!" But instead Jesus addressed his attitude and said: "Be of *good cheer*." Why might he have done this? Why would Jesus tell the man to cheer up before giving him any physical reason to be happy? Well, Jesus gives us the answer to that question. He tells the man, "Be of good cheer because your sins are forgiven." The reason he gave the man for being cheerful was that he had forgiven his sins. Only later was he healed (which was another reason to be cheerful), but this was secondary to the excitement he must have felt for being for-given and given access to a relationship with the Father. Christ never told people to be glad without giving them a great reason to cheer up. And Jesus never gave anyone a shallow reason to be happy. Instead he addressed the deepest depravity of their soul and set them free. That is a reason to be cheerful!

Many of our attempts to encourage others are weak and powerless. To a friend who is moping around feeling sorry for themselves we say, "Come on dude, snap out of it, its not that bad." He responds, "You just don't understand, I have no reason to be happy right now."

We need to get to the root of what's going on here. You and I cannot say to our friend, as Christ did: "Your sins are forgiven." But we can say, "Cheer up. Do you realize how much God loves you? He is near to you and will carry your burden if you just give it to him."

You may not be able to convince him this is true, but at least you have given him some real reason to cheer up. And you have not made things worse by just patting him on the back and speaking hollow words that don't give him any real hope in the midst of his depression.

Lets look at another example of how Christ truly cheered people up. One time, a woman who had been bleeding for a long time came to him, full of faith that she would be healed. When she got close enough to Jesus to touch him, she reached out and grasped his garment. Then came the surprise. Jesus said to her, "Daughter, be of *good cheer*." Why did he say this to someone who had been through years of such heart-wrenching pain? Jesus didn't give people canned clichés. Rather, he was telling her to cheer up because, by God's grace, her *faith* had made her well! "Your faith has saved you." (see Luke 7:50)

Christ never tells us to be joyful unless there is some great reason for joy. And his reasons usually go beyond mere physical welfare.

Here is another great example of Jesus speaking into the depths of someone's soul to cheer them up. I cannot say it any better than another author who commented on this encounter:

You remember the scene–our Lord alone on the mountain in prayer, the darkness coming down upon the little boat, the storm rising as the darkness fell, the wind howling down the gorges of the mountains round the land-locked lake, the crew toiling in rowing, for the wind was against them! And then, all at once, out of the mysterious obscurity beneath the shadows of the hill, something is seen moving. It comes nearer: and the waves become solid beneath that light and noiseless foot, as steadily he comes. Jesus Christ uses the waves as the pavement on which he approaches his servants, and the storms, which beat on us are his occasion for drawing very near.

Then they think he is a spirit. They cry out with a shriek of terror—because Jesus Christ is coming to them in so strange a fashion! And when he comes it is with those same words on his lips, 'Be of good cheer.'

Tell us not to be frightened when we see something walking across the waves in the darkness! 'It is I.' Surely that is enough. The Companion in the storm is the Calmer of the terror. He who recognizes Jesus Christ as drawing near to his heart over windy waves may well 'be of good cheer' since the storm but brings his truest Treasure to him.[12]

Again in John chapter 16 we read how Christ, who was at the very end of his earthly life, tells his disciples about his death and predicts their cowardly betrayal and desertion. Then he ends his talk with these gracious words: "In the world you will have tribulation, but *be of good cheer.* I have overcome the world." (see John 16:33 ASV)

Make sure you don't miss the reason Jesus gives for why they should be cheerful: "I have overcome the world." He seems to be saying: "As you trust in *me* for your strength you can overcome your fears."

Jesus used similar words to lift the Apostle Paul's soul while he was stuck in the prison in Caesarea. Jesus had already returned to the right hand of the Father in heaven, but now he sees how much Paul needs encouragement. Paul was in danger of being "torn to pieces" by a group of infuriated Jews. So Jesus speaks to him: "But the following night the Lord stood by him and said, 'Be of good cheer, Paul; for as you have testified for Me in Jerusalem, so you must also bear witness at Rome." (see Acts 23:11 NKJV)

I am so glad these words were recorded in the Bible so we could benefit from them. Because it shows that not only did Christ speak this way to his disciples while he was on earth, but he also uses the same language from the heavens to us today: "Be of good cheer!"

How many millions of times, has Christ uttered these words through the Holy Spirit to Believers throughout history? Imagine all of the souls that have anguished in times of trouble; people, who have been overcome by sorrow: Men, women, and children who have been sick, or even the ones who have lost their worldly possessions. "Be of good cheer. I am alive. All is not lost. With me you have all things."

This even became a favorite saying of the Apostle Paul. In the midst of the great shipwreck off the coast of Malta recorded in the book of Acts, Luke writes: "When all hope that we should be saved was now taken away,' he exhorted the crew to be of *'good cheer*,'" and again in the next verse, "…Sirs, be of *good cheer*." And as it turns out, his encouragement was effective. Even before the ship struck the reef and broke up, they followed his example and took food and "were all of *good cheer*." (see Acts 27)

The Apostle's words were not shallow or empty. They were based on the message of deliverance he had received from an angel of God, "to whom I belong and whom I serve."

Young friends, especially if you are a Christian, I want to encourage you that you can always share a word of good cheer to others, because you are drawing upon the resources of Christ. You are pointing others to him for comfort. Ours is a faith of "good cheer" because we have a Savior who can ultimately cheer people up! You can always say enthusiastically to others, "Take your eyes off of yourself, God will cheer you up." Even better than that, you can always remind your friends, "God is not only in the heavens; he is actively involved in our life right now."[13]

Jesus was conscious at all times of his Father's presence. This is why in loneliness, poverty, or when he was betrayed, mocked, misunderstood, deserted, hated, beaten, and eventually killed; Jesus was able to remain cheerful. Today he offers you and I the same source of joy, for he was and is the Lord of Good Cheer.

DISCUSSION QUESTIONS

1. Why do you think Jesus was able to be cheerful through the circumstances of his life?
2. What are some examples of when Jesus used the expression, "Be of good cheer?"
3. What is an example of a person in the Gospels using this phrase?
4. What are some reasons you can think of that we can be cheerful even when things are not going well?
5. In what ways does the story of Jesus walking on the water comfort you?
6. How might Christ's promises of future joy provide relief when you feel sorrowful?
7. Give an example of when the Apostle Paul used the same words when he in serious danger.
8. Do you think we too have the same ability to be cheerful in the midst of hardship?
9. Share some personal examples of how you have seen someone who loves Christ remain joyful in the midst of great trial. Why do you think they were able to remain cheerful?

CHAPTER 10

TACTFUL

♦ ♦ ♦

SO MANY WELL-INTENTIONED PEOPLE DAMAGE relationships by not having any tact. A careless word, or a gesture of impatience can easily invalidate the many good words you may have spoken to someone. In the same way that love covers over a multitude of sins, lack of tact can spoil a multitude of good deeds:

> Evil is wrought by lack of thought,
> As well as by lack of heart.[14]

Sometimes we say people who have no tact just "have thick skin." Yet having thick skin is not really an indicator of kindness, is it? Ignoring other people's feelings or cultural traditions is not a sign of strength at all. As the saying goes, "A bull in a china closet will break the dishes." Actually, when it comes to leadership, you don't want any bulls in your china closet. In other words, you don't want people on your student ministry team who lack *tact*.

Tactlessness is not usually something young people struggle with. Yet when adults gain some maturity and life experience, they are often tempted to think more highly of themselves then they ought to. Without regard for other people's opinions, a tactless person will likely become too blunt. This kind of callousness is the opposite of tactfulness. For example, the tactless parent might squelch his children so much that they won't feel free to share their feelings or a difference of opinion with them. A tactless husband will intimidate his wife so much that she won't even dare to disagree with him. His neighbors probably won't even want to talk with him because they don't want to be beaten over the head with his opinions. Instead, avoiding any chance of getting into an argument, they will avoid him. A tactless person is extremely disliked, although people might not directly tell him they don't like him.

Perhaps people like this should be described by a harsher word than "tactless." Nevertheless, the issue here is that when people lack sensitivity and ignore the rights and feelings of others, their lack of tact tears down relationships.

Tactlessness comes in other forms as well. Some people are just plain conceited and their large ego causes them to bulldoze people's feelings. A person I know can hardly talk about anything other than himself. He draws attention to his success, he brags about his verbal prowess to win arguments, his charitable giving, his most recent speaking engagements, how he mesmerized his audience, etc. He is completely ignorant that others could care less.[15]

Sometimes tactless people come across as downright mean. This person takes pride in his bluntness and doesn't care if it hurts others. To him, being right is the supreme goal. He actually takes pleasure in seeing his helpless victims shrink back from his superior knowledge. People who treat others this way distinctly turn off young people.

To a young person, if you are tactless, then you must be a bit heartless too. It doesn't matter if the real issue is just careless disregard for other people's opinions... young people will just reject tactless people as irrelevant. For example, a tactless person might make the joking comment, "Who is that guy that looks like a baboon?" And then the person next to him says, "That is my twin brother..." The tactless person might try to back track and say, "Oh please forgive me, that was really a dumb thing to say...." At that point it is too late... the tactless person is dismissed as a complete dork. Young people, especially, won't want to have anything to do with him.

We have all probably at some time caused someone to be embarrassed or angry because of a tactless comment. Usually this makes us feel really bad. But I wonder what a difference it would make if more Believers considered tactfulness as a Christian virtue? In reality, this is just the case. Jesus Christ showed tactfulness on many occasions. And this is another reason why I believe young people are especially drawn to his personality.

I have already mentioned his conversation with the Samaritan woman. Yet I can't think of a better example of tactfulness than this incredible encounter. It would have been really easy for Jesus to say something that would have made her feel defensive. But if he had said something too blunt, she probably would have walked away, and he would have missed an opportunity to teach her (and the rest of the world) such a profound eternal truth.

First of all, Jesus shows us his tactfulness in the way he simply asks her for a favor: "Will you give me a drink? (see John 4:7) If you think about it, asking someone for some help can bridge a relationship even better than offering to help them. To receive something from someone is an offer of grace. Sometimes in our pride we can offer help to others, whereas it requires genuine humility to ask someone for help.

It is noticeably tactful the way Jesus didn't take offense at the woman's awkward question in response to his humble request: "You are a Jew and I am a Samaritan woman. How can you ask me for a drink? (For Jews do not associate with Samaritans.)" (see John 4:9) A person with less patience would have probably answered her, "Really? Why do you care about my ethnicity? I just need a drink of water." Yet instead of responding like this, Christ suggested that there was actually some other kind of water that he could offer her that was much more satisfying than the water in the bottom of Jacob's well.

Even though Jesus only needed a drink of water to satisfy his parched tongue, he recognized this was an opportunity for evangelism which was much more important than his thirst at that moment. Quickly he realized that this woman was probably not going to understand what this "Living Water" was that he was talking about. So he took a more tactful approach.

"Sir,' the woman said, 'you have nothing to draw with and the well is deep. Where can you get this living water? Are you greater than our father Jacob, who gave us the well and drank from it himself, as did also his sons and his livestock?" (see John 4:11-12) A really thirsty person may have lost his patience and just drawn the water for himself. Yet Christ, put aside his thirst and any natural impatience, and pursued her heart. He took the opportunity to lead her to the Living Water (which she needed much more than he needed a drink).

Ironically we don't even know if Jesus got a drink of water at all. At the end of their interaction, the woman left her water pot (apparently in her excitement she forgot why she had come to the well), and "went back to town," to tell all of her friends and neighbors about meeting this wonderful stranger.

But before she left him, Christ again displayed his tactfulness by not drawing unnecessary attention to her sinful life. Instead he said, "Go, call your husband and come back." This led her to confess, "I have no husband," though she was fully aware that she had been with five husbands.

All of this conversation led up to the woman's revelation that this was actually the Messiah in her presence; "I, the one speaking to you—I am he." (see John 4:26) This was a discovery that she probably could not have understood without the tactful conversation that led up to it, and the illumination of the Holy Spirit which helped her understand that what Jesus was saying was true.

I am not sure that it is generally a good idea, when first meeting a stranger, to say something like, "How would you like to become a Christian?" Even though there is far more danger in not asking this question compared to asking it in the wrong way. It is still better to lead up to this question tactfully and naturally, like Jesus led up to the proclamation that he was the Messiah to this Samaritan woman.

Let's look at one more example to illustrate the tactfulness of Christ. In this account, he shows great tact and discretion in dealing with a woman caught in the act of adultery. This was a clear case. The law was straightforward, and her guilt was apparently unquestionable. Jesus could have probably taken a few different approaches in this situation. First, he could have taken sides with her accusers and said, "The law is the law. She is a sinful woman, and she must face the consequences of her sin." I wonder how many of us would have taken this approach, pointing the finger at her and standing in judgment. But this strategy would not have caused her to *want* to "sin no more." It would have probably heightened her sense of abandonment.

He might also have avoided the Pharisees' trap by saying, "This is no concern of mine. I have more important things to do than to settle this case." Yet if he had done that, this crucial lesson would have not been learned. Neither the woman's nor the crowd's consciences would have been pricked, and it might have led the woman to think that he made light of the sin.

He didn't choose either of these options. Instead, he stooped down and wrote on the ground. He probably did this to emphasize his point. And in doing so, the whole crowd became still. The uproar against the poor woman was hushed for a moment. Then he lifted his eyes, and said, "Let any one of you who is without sin be the first to throw a stone at her." (see John 8:7) And again he bent down and wrote on the ground.

Stooping down was a tactful way to give both the woman's accusers and the woman herself a chance to retreat. Jesus cared both for the woman and the crowd. If he had set his eyes on the crowd, they would probably have not felt the freedom to leave like they did. Their pride would have compelled them to defend their self-righteous judgment upon the woman. But with no eye upon them, and only their consciences accusing them, "Those who heard began to go away one at a time." Ironically, the oldest people left first. They got the point.

When he looked up again, only the woman was left. She and Jesus were alone. Rather than running away in embarrassment she stood their waiting to hear what Jesus would say. With his pure eyes upon her, he gently forgave her for the sin she committed. We can assume she repented and obeyed his command to, "Go and sin no more."

The tactfulness that Jesus displayed in managing this situation was truly amazing. The Scribes and Pharisees didn't get to have it their way. Nor did they achieve their goal of finding a way to accuse him. The woman was not jaded further in her sin by being treated harshly, nor was she let off the hook for her sin. Christ avoided the Pharisees' trap. They wanted to accuse him of disobedience to Moses' law. He also avoided making the woman even more miserable. Instead he showed her love and forgiveness. The weapons his enemies used against him came back on their own heads, like a boomerang.

By reflecting on this one incident, one could never accuse Jesus of being judgmental. On the contrary, the tact he displayed in this situation shows us the depth of his love for sinners and accusers alike.

DISCUSSION QUESTIONS

1. In your own words, what is tactfulness? Is it worth developing in your own life? What are some reasons why?

2. Write down some ways that you might be able to show more tactfulness in your relationships.

3. Re-tell in your own words the story of the Samaritan woman. In what ways was Jesus tactful with her? Identify some things that she said or did that might have irritated the average person. What are some untactful things that he could have said to her?

4. How did Jesus lead the conversation with the Samaritan woman toward revealing that he was the Messiah? Following Jesus' example, what are some things we learn from this story about good ways to approach people in regard to their personal beliefs or religion?

5. Retell in your own words the story of Jesus and the woman caught in adultery. How might he have avoided this uncomfortable situation?

6. What do you think are some reasons why he wrote with his finger on the ground? In what ways did this action display the amazing tactfulness of Jesus?

7. In your own words, what was the outcome of this event with the sinful woman and the crowd?

8. What are some of the other character qualities this story reveals about Jesus?

CHAPTER 11

AN UNCOMPLAINING HERO

♦ ♦ ♦

OF ALL PEOPLE WHO YOUNG people want to avoid, it is a complaining whiner. Nagging drains the life out of young people. It throws a wet blanket on their optimism and willingness to risk. Young people stay clear of nagging adults. Instead, young people's heroes are people who do their work without complaining. Their heroes do heroic deeds without ever showing off their battle wounds. It is way too common today that men and woman feel so sorry for themselves. They want everyone to know that their problems are bigger than everyone else's; their troubles more troublesome, their hardships are more difficult than those of others.[16]

A woman once said to me, "I think I have suffered more than any other woman who's ever lived." What a ridiculous statement of self-pity! Think about the sufferings of the martyrs and bold confessors of the faith. What about Jesus' mother Mary who had to watch her son die on a cross? Or how about the suffering of Joan of Arc, or Charlotte Corday?[17] These women's suffering does not even compare to the light and momentary suffering of the woman I was talking to.

Many of us, when we suffer, think that we have it much worse than others. But we soon realize, when the trial is over that nothing has happened to us but that which is common to others. The difficult thing to do when suffering from anxiety or worry is to keep from feeling sorry for ourselves and complaining of our situation.

The truly heroic person will be strong and uncomplaining when things go wrong, when friends abandon them, or when enemies mock them. Jesus measured up to this standard of heroism.

He lived thirty years in an insignificant rural village that was way off the beaten path. Even though from his boyhood he probably had glimpses of his significant mission ahead, he never seems to have gotten frustrated over the long delay before he could begin his active ministry. So many people are impatient if their job isn't just perfect or if it is taking too long to rise to some place of recognition in their company. Even many pastors are discontent with their small church or their minimal opportunities to influence the world. Yet they forget that Jesus, who came to minister to the whole world, was thirty years old before he preached his first sermon or did his first public work.

Many young doctors curse the long, long years of struggle before they get their first chance to practice medicine or actually get a decent paycheck for their expertise.

Jesus can certainly relate with those who are patiently waiting to spread their wings. The town Jesus grew up in, Nazareth, was not only an obscure place but the people of this area were also unresponsive to him when he finally began his ministry. You probably could not have picked a more obscure place for him to start his ministry. The people of Nazareth were so slow to acknowledge his claims that even when he became famous for performing miracles, he was still "a prophet without honor in his hometown." In fact, much to his dismay, the Nazarenes lashed out against him, dragging him to the edge of cliff to throw him over because he rebuked their hardness of heart.

But we never hear any complaints from him. He expressed no outrage against Nazareth, even though they totally deserved it.

One of the hardest things for a uniquely talented person to handle is to be misunderstood by his nearest relatives or to be despised or disapproved by them. But this cross, too, Jesus had to bear: "For even his own brothers did not believe in him." (see John 7:5) Yet without complaint, he put up with people's unbelief until at last James, and probably his other brothers, eventually became his loyal disciples.

Jesus' poverty and homelessness must have been another hard trial to bear. Yet we hear no complaint or self-pity. One time Jesus shared what he thought about his homelessness: "Foxes have dens and birds have nests, but the Son of Man has no place to lay his head." (see Luke 9:58) Instead of complaining, he writes a poem about it! He simply states the fact that the Father wanted him to be homeless so his impact could reach further throughout Palestine.

Another bitter pill Jesus had to take was the constant dullness and inconsistency of his friends. There is probably not anything more exasperating to a servant leader than to be constantly misunderstood. But people constantly had wrong ideas about what Jesus was doing. For example, Peter, Thomas and John often failed to catch the meaning of what he was saying. And they for sure didn't grasp his mission for a long time. A normal man would probably have snapped at them and rebuked them for their ignorance and lack of faith. But we hear none of that from Jesus' lips. Instead, he was courteous and gentle in his responses, always displaying unusual patience. There was one time that he exclaimed, "How foolish you are, and how slow to believe," to a group of unbelievers, but it was not the expression of any personal annoyance. He was just in awe that they didn't believe what the *prophets* had written.

And at the end of his life, his enemies unfairly poured out their wrath on him even though he had done no wrong. Yet Jesus didn't get moody or condemn them. He intentionally didn't reprimand them for their cruelty, but showed them pity instead: "Father, forgive them, for they do not know what they are doing." (see Luke 23:34)

Just as the miracles displayed Jesus' Divine nature, so his self-control and gentle, uncomplaining heroism proved that he was most certainly God in the flesh.

I have a friend who has been partially paralyzed for nearly twenty years. Little by little the disease has been creeping up to his brain. One after another, his feet, hands, back, and tongue, have slowly lost their functionality. But I have never heard a word of complaint from him. His devoted wife has waited on him tirelessly during all these years and she does not groan in self-pity at all. Then tragically she had an accident that sent her to the hospital. Sadly, she lost one of her feet and now must use crutches to get around while she cares for her husband. Before his disease set in, he was a brilliant leader and a beloved and successful pastor. Yet with all of this suffering, and now all of his opportunities to lead and influence people diminished and with all of the hopes they had seemingly shattered, this man and woman have one of the most joyful homes that I know of. The last time I heard from my friend's wife, she said that even though he cannot speak anymore, "We still have such good times together. We have never been happier."

As I walk away from the bedside of my friend, I come away with a greater sense that I have been with a hero. Heroes are not just those who win battles or save thousands of lives from burning buildings. My friend is so uncomplaining and unconcerned with himself. This is the very essence of heroism.

This is the lesson Jesus Christ teaches us about the love which, "suffers long, and is kind," the love which, "always protects, always trusts, always hopes, always perseveres." (see 1 Corinthians 13:4-7) Such is the uncomplaining heroic personality of our Master, Jesus Christ.

DISCUSSION QUESTIONS

1. Make a long list of personality qualities that young people appreciate in others. If you are a young person, be honest about what qualities attract you to someone. If you are an adult, ask a few young people what personality qualities they are especially drawn to. Give some examples of people you know who have those qualities.

2. What do you think is sinful about complaining? In what ways does complaining erode a person's character?

3. Share some of what we learned from the Bible about the first thirty years of Jesus' life.

4. Realizing Jesus' divine mission, why do you think he wasn't worried at all about his seemingly unnoticed, humble years in Nazareth?

5. What do you think it was like for him to grow up in Nazareth?

6. What did he say about his peasant lifestyle? Why do you think he didn't complain about it?

7. How did Jesus treat his friends and disciples who constantly misunderstood him?

8. What were some of Jesus' last words about his enemies?

9. Why do you think Jesus didn't complain? How do you think you can become more like Christ in this personality trait?

10. Read 1 Corinthians 13. What does the Apostle Paul say about complaining? What is a small step you can take to grow in this area?

CHAPTER 12

COMMITTED

◆ ◆ ◆

A PERSON WHO IS NOT committed to anything does not shape the world. We all recognize apathetic people. They have figured out how to worm their way through life, avoiding responsibility, refusing to do the hard things, never finishing what they start. When adults are not committed, young people are not impressed. They admire people who display commitment. This gives them an example to follow.

No writer ever penned a truer principle about apathetic people than the Apostle James who wrote, "Such a person is double-minded and unstable in all they do." (see James 1:8)

Dependability is at the root of all Christian integrity. It is equally true that inconsistency is a sure sign of weak character. Young people are naturally drawn to people who display dependability and consistency.

When a person decides to follow Christ, he does not say, "I'm going to try out being a disciple for a month and if I like it I'll continue on." Seeking to become like Christ is not an experiment. It has to be the utmost goal of your life. Your primary calling is to abide in him and grow in his likeness.

The Master never accepts conditional allegiance. He knows your heart. To be a Christian is to decide once and for all that Christ is the King of your life now and forever.

As the Christian Endeavour Movement pledge puts it, "I promise him that I will strive to do whatever he would like me do, and *throughout my whole life* I will endeavour to lead a Christian life." How weak and inadequate it would be if it said, "I will try to grow in Christ-likeness for the next ten days," or "When I feel like it, I will be loyal to Christ."

And yet this is what many so-called Christians pledge to Christ. While the "spiritual high" lasts, while emotion is at its peak (in other words while they feel like it), they enjoy abiding in Christ. Jesus described these disloyal types with unflattering detail in the Parable of the Sower and the Seeds. There are some who hear the word but the seed of truth was not planted in deep soil. When the sun arose with scorching heat, the little sprouts (even though they had good intention) eventually withered away. In other words, they lacked commitment.

Relationships rely on persistent commitment. A true friend is one who is loyal and devoted. What is marriage worth if a couple is not dedicated to one another? One of the most grievous evils of our day is divorce, which simply demonstrates conditional love and lack of faithfulness to the promises that were made in their wedding vows. What is a treaty between nations if it is merely torn up (as often as they have been) on the whim of changing politics?

No, the foundation stone of business, religion, family life and politics is *commitment*.

Let's consider for a moment how Jesus illustrated this great virtue in his very first recorded statement: "I must be about my Father's business." (see Luke 2:49) Even then at twelve-years-old, Jesus had glimpses of his life work. He never deviated from it, all the way to his crucifixion.

Over and over he repeated the same thought: "As long as it is day, we must do the works of him who sent me. Night is coming, when no one can work." (see John 9:4) Even up to the moment he cried out with his last breath, "It is finished," he remained committed to his life work.

Suppose that Jesus had for a moment forgotten his purpose, or lost his enthusiasm for it. Suppose that some intense opposition had discouraged him, or that the thought of the cross had riddled him with fear! Suppose the Devil had gotten the better of him through temptation. What would have been the consequences to mankind? Imagine a world without a Savior. Try to envision an unredeemed humanity; an earth completely ruled by the Devil. All that we are or ever hope to be depends upon our Savior's commitment to the mission the Father gave him to accomplish.

Consider how devoted he was to his friends. He chose Peter, James and John at the beginning of his public ministry. Yet when they were with him at Golgotha, they stood at a distance, probably because they were afraid. This seeming lack of commitment on their part did not effect Jesus' commitment to them.

The dependability and loyalty of Jesus' friendship was the glue that bound this unstable group of disciples together. Even Peter, the most temperamental and fickle of all, could not stay for long outside of the circle of Jesus' compelling, steadfast love, even when he felt ashamed for betraying him.

Every one of the Disciples was transformed by this kind of loyal friendship except one sad exception, Judas the traitor. Even Christ's unmeasured love could not overcome Judas' greed.

And think for a moment of the way in which the Disciple's love for the Master has inspired the steadfast devotion of followers of Christ through the centuries ever since that agonizing day on the cross. Those timid boys before the resurrection became bold men immediately afterwards. We read no more of a hesitant, double-minded Peter. We no longer see an overly sensitive John. As far as we know, every one of the disciples remained true to the end.

According to church tradition, James was the first one of the Disciples to be martyred. Peter even asked to be crucified upside down so that he might suffer an even more dishonorable death than his Master. John, who lived to a ripe old age, looked across the waves from his island prison in Patmos to his beloved seven churches in Asia. All of these men's lives tell us something about how their lives were shaped by their Master's heroic commitment to them.

And think about how many millions of people have demonstrated unshakable devotion to Jesus throughout history. In a tomb on the heights of the great city of Smyrna, (in modern-day Turkey) lie the bones of Polycarp. He was one of the earliest Christian martyrs. His last memorable words which have echoed down the centuries were uttered when he was about to be beheaded and was asked to renounce his faith in Christ. He said, "Eighty and six years have I served him, and he has never done me wrong: How can I deny him now?"

In substance, these words have been echoed by countless martyrs from that early century down to the events like the Boxer rebellion in 1900 where hundreds of missionaries and thousands of Chinese Christians gave their lives for their faith.

In an ancient coastal town of Aigues Mortes, France is a great stone tower, called the "Tower of Constance." In this tower were imprisoned many Huguenot Protestants after the edict of Nantes was revoked. Among the prisoners was a young girl who was imprisoned when she was twelve years old because her brother was a Protestant pastor. For thirty-four long years she was confined in this stone dungeon, but she would not renounce her faith. While living out her years in isolation, she scratched with her needle in the stone floor the one French word, "Resistez," which means, "Resist." For two hundred years that word has inspired other Christians. I have gathered with a large group of young people in the Student Endeavour Movement around that stone and thanked God for her example of loyal affection for Jesus. This demonstration of commitment to Jesus is unconquerable. It is deathless.

DISCUSSION QUESTIONS

1. What are some reasons why commitment is essential to the success of a mission?

2. Why do you think it is not possible to become a Christian tentatively or conditionally, or with a time limit?

3. Share in your own words the Parable of the Sower and the Seeds and how it describes a wavering, disloyal Believer.

4. In what kinds of relationships is commitment absolutely necessary? How does commitment make those relationships better?

5. How did Jesus as a boy express the steadfast purpose of his life?

6. Share in your own words the story of the temptation in the wilderness. What does this show about Jesus' devotion? (see Matthew 4:1-11)

7. What are some ways Jesus showed he was committed to his friends?

8. How did Jesus inspire dedication and devotion in others?

9. Retell the story of Aigues Mortes. What are some things this story teaches us?

CHAPTER 13

IDEALISTIC

♦ ♦ ♦

ANY TYPICAL YOUNG PERSON, WHO has been brought up in a normal environment, is going to be somewhat idealistic. For some young people these ideals may be more dreams than reality. But it is normal for young people to have an idealistic view of life.

I would venture to say that one of the reasons why teenagers are so attracted to Jesus is because he had such lofty aspirations.

Adults so easily forget how important it is to encourage young people to dream big. We may not understand their dreams and they may even seem impossible to attain, but it is crucial for student ministry leaders to admire young people for their optimism.

To understand the idealism of our Master, it is only necessary to study carefully the Beatitudes in the fifth chapter of Matthew and the sixth chapter of Luke. During all the nineteen centuries since they were spoken, no higher standard of human action has ever been proposed. And people still fall way short of reaching the standards of the Beatitudes. This has caused some to even think that Christ's standards are impractical or even impossible to achieve. They've missed the point.

Think for a moment of the people in the Beatitudes who are called the "blessed" ones. The "poor in spirit" are blessed; those who are not pushy or prideful, but those who are ready to surrender their will to God are considered blessed.

Those who "mourn" are blessed. These are people we are supposed to feel sorry for. But according to Jesus, if they mourn for their sins they are the ones who "will be comforted."

The "meek," are also blessed. But gentleness and submissiveness are almost terms of disgrace these days. Yet Christ dared to say that they will "inherit the earth." Those who retaliate are not blessed, nor are those who demand an eye for an eye and a tooth for a tooth. Yet those who turn the other cheek, people who bless those who curse them, and those who pray for the ones who insult them are the ones whom Jesus says will be blessed.

"Blessed are the peacemakers," he says, and yet after all these centuries the nations keep coming way short of his high standard. The bloodiest war of all time is being waged as these words are written.

I don't need to recite the rest of the Beatitudes: but you should know that they are ideas of the highest caliber. I would urge my readers to read them again and again, until you comprehend these awesome ideal standards of human conduct and make them your own.

But you might say, "What is the use of having such ideals for mankind if we can't ever reach them? After nearly two thousand years, we are as far away from them as ever. Wouldn't it be better to have lower ideals that we could actually achieve?" This is false and destructive reasoning. We can see from the study of history how lower ideals have affected mankind. Muslims have ideals. Some of them are noble, like their standards of total abstinence, fasting, and their call to prayer. But at the end of the day, Jesus expressed even the higher goals than these in the Sermon on the Mount. Buddha had standards, and his followers have sought to realize them. He proposed goals of calmness and indifference to worldly concerns. He believed it was best to make your mind and spirit callous toward hope, fear and grief so that you wouldn't cause anyone else to suffer. But even these standards fall short of the ideals expressed in the Sermon on the Mount.

The great ideals of Confucius are worthy of consideration, for they include reverence and respect for older people. He taught the importance of honoring one's parents and ancestors. All of these are noble qualities but they seem so limited and powerless compared with the larger and vastly higher ideals of Jesus. Even if you lump in all of the "good" of every religion, Jesus' ideal vision for humanity was enormously greater.

Ideals have power. The ideals of Muhammad, Buddha and Confucius have influenced vast populations of the human race. They have made Turkey and the Arab world what they are, and the Orient what it is today.

And yet, however largely Christ's ideals have influenced the Christian world, it is again necessary to remind ourselves how far short we all have come toward achieving them. Every generation sees these perfect standards from afar, but struggles to even approach them. Yet however slight our attempts have been, and however far away from the goal we are, these ideal standards and ethics of Jesus have done a world of good for humanity. They have abolished the slave trade and slavery. They have condemned suicide and unjust war. They have discouraged people from giving in to the temptations every kind of lust that seeks to destroy people. They have encouraged freedom, and they have promoted the peaceful standards of the Golden Rule; to "Do to others as you would have them do to you."

Young people let me ask you a question. In your thoughtful and honest moments, would you have any other ideals than those that are recorded in these two great chapters of the New Testament? Would you choose to have a world with any lower standards of what is right and wrong than what Jesus spoke about? Even though these standards make you and I feel bad when we break them or they may seem impossible to reach, would you rather have any other Leader who expected less or promoted any lesser ideals than those that the life and teachings of Jesus have established for all mankind?

DISCUSSION QUESTIONS

1. Do you think from your own experience that young people generally have high ideals and big dreams? What are some examples?

2. What are some Scripture passages where the ideals of Jesus are taught?

3. Do you think the Beatitudes are impossible to live out today?

4. Is an unreached ideal or goal worthless? If not, why not?

5. How are nations and politics affected by religious ideals? Compare some of the different values of Judeo-Christian, Muslim, and Buddhist cultures.

6. What practical results have the standards and ideals of Christ accomplished already in the world?

7. Do you think wars will ever cease? Explain your reason for believing this.

8. Do you think the world will ever see the damage done to families, marriages, and relationships by alcoholism, abuse, and divorce reduced or ceased?

9. In your opinion, is the Golden Rule the highest standard of mankind? Why or why not?

CHAPTER 14

WHAT DO YOU THINK OF JESUS?

♦ ♦ ♦

WE HAVE BEEN CONSIDERING THE winsome appeal of Jesus to the young people of every generation. The young can see in Jesus those personality qualities that excite and inspire them to change the world. We have discovered that he was totally authentic. Young people are always drawn to those who are genuine. They are repelled by a fake.

We have seen the approachability of Christ, as well as his courage and generous affection for others. All of these qualities are characteristics that young people are attracted to. He was quite non-traditional, he was considerate of people's feelings and his tactfulness and wittiness confounded the "wisdom" of his enemies. He was committed, never complained, and constantly cheerful. He was not afraid to call people to the highest standards of living.

All these personality qualities naturally appeal to young people. They just need someone to give them an accurate picture of Jesus. Christ is the epitome of every young person's hero. He is their example to follow.

We have learned of his simplicity and his approachability. He was a humble peasant among peasants, an obedient son, and a humble loyal friend. Yet it is almost startling to hear the claims that he makes of himself. If his lifestyle had made him look arrogant, prideful or full of himself, then we would not be surprised to hear him say, "I am the Way, the Truth and the Life, no man can come to the Father accept through me." No greater claims have ever been made by any man; no such self-assertion has ever been dreamed of by any mere man outside of an insane asylum. Not even the world's most ruthless conquerors have claimed, "I and my Father are one."

Perhaps some readers who know their Bibles really well might remind me that in another place Jesus says, "My Father is greater than I." But this seeming contradiction is only another proof that he is who he claimed to be. Think of Alexander the Great, or Napoleon, or Kaiser Wilhelm, saying in all seriousness, "God is greater than I am." Such a statement, comparing oneself to God, would either show that the man was out of his head, or it would be such a colossal piece of egotism that few world conquerors would have ever dared to utter it.

But it was the meek and lowly Jesus that said this; the modest friend of tax collectors and sinners; the Carpenter of Nazareth. We can understand these two seeming contradictions when we remember the relationship between a father and his son. The father and son in the ideal family are one: they are one in sympathy, one in purpose, one in deepest affection.

Yet the father, simply because he is father, is greater than the son. Jesus does not stop to explain his words in this case. He seldom does. But his claim that God the Father is greater than God the Son (himself) is, by implication, as strong a statement of his unique Divine nature as could possibly be made. There are no contradictions in Jesus.

Again he says, "The Queen of the South will rise at the judgment with this generation and condemn it; for she came from the ends of the earth to listen to Solomon's wisdom, and now something greater than Solomon is here." (see Matthew 12:42) That, to be sure, is a modest statement compared with the words we have just quoted. But even that would be a statement that few kings in their royal robes would dare to make. But Jesus Christ our Lord said this, and who would question or doubt his statement?

Again he says, "Whoever acknowledges me before others, I will also acknowledge before my Father in heaven." (see Matthew 10:32) What mere man, outside of being crazy would ever dare to say such things? And if someone did say this, they would be laughed at.

Recall for an instant the parable of the man who built his house upon the sand. Who does Jesus say that this man is like in our modern world? He is the man who hears Christ's sayings or reads them, and does not follow them. According to Jesus, that man's house will be destroyed. Yet the man who hears and obeys Christ's teaching is the man who builds his house upon the rock. Even the rain and the wind will not destroy that house. Jesus was claiming that his teaching is the foundational rock for all men. He himself is the Rock on which one should build his life.

If Jesus was only a man and said these kinds of things, we would have to consider him quite self-centered. Even the wisest philosophers and the greatest authors never dared to make such a claim.

Such words would sound foolish in the mouth of Homer, Shakespeare, or Milton. Yet the world has acknowledged that Jesus had the right to say what he said. His life was perfectly congruent.

As we consider Jesus' claims about himself we only have two options. Either Christ was who he said he was, the unique Son of God, one with the Father, the Way, the Truth and the Life, the Vine of which we are the branches, the One greater than Solomon, and the foundation Rock of human character, or he was the most conceited, full-of-himself lunatic the world has ever seen. Human nature cannot let us accept this second alternative. Few people have ever seriously held the belief that Jesus was a crazy narcissist. Even Christ's enemies have avoided saying things like that after reading the story of his life and sacrificial death.

So now that you have been given an accurate picture of Jesus. If you are a thoughtful young person and you have considered what Jesus said and did from these stories in the Bible, who would you say Jesus is? Have you been drawn or attracted to his personality like I have been? What is your response to him other than to cry out like what one of Jesus' doubting disciples finally did when he realized who Jesus really was: "My Lord and My God!"

DISCUSSION QUESTIONS

1. In your own words, what are some of the personality traits you have learned about Jesus?
2. Share some of the things you think young people are most idealistic about. Compare this list to what you hear and see in Jesus. What do these two lists have in common?
3. What are some of the claims Jesus made about himself? Has any sane man that you know of ever made such claims?
4. From what we've read in this chapter, how do you explain Christ's seemingly arrogant statement, "The Father is greater than I"? How could he have had the audacity to compare himself to God?
5. What are some other astonishing statements Jesus made about himself?
6. Since Jesus Christ made these statements, what are the only two possible conclusions about his identity?
7. What do you think of Jesus Christ? Share in your own words who you think Jesus is, and whether you desire to become one of his disciples.

END NOTES

1. "If an evangelist comes to town, if a Billy Sunday moves a city to its depths, young people are expected to flock to the front and profess conversion."
2. "This does not do away with the idea of conversion, or substitute confession or confirmation for regeneration;"
3. "...as were Paul's and Jerry McAuley's". Jerry McAuley was radically transformed later in life by reading the Bible while in prison at Sing Sing in the 1860's. He later became the founder of the New York City Rescue Mission in 1872.
4. "Where there is one Jerry McAuley, there are a hundred who may scarce remember the time when they were not Christians because they met Christ when they were young."
5. "This is unfortunately demonstrated in some of your colleges and high schools, when a sincere, outspoken Christian is looked upon as a freak or an oddball, who would for instance, be kept out of many college fraternities unless, by chance, he happened to perform well on the football field or the baseball diamond."
6. "The childhood miracles recorded in the Apocryphal writings are not recorded in the Gospels, so we can assume they are just myths."
7. "The invitation even tells you what kind of clothes you should wear. In my experience, it is best to wear a business suit, but the king's representative would specifically tell me

---

the requirements for the cut of my coat, the color of my gloves and tie, and the style of my hat. And the king or emperor would usually receive me in uniform to show that it is a state ceremony and not a social call that he grants."

8. "There are so many instances we could quote, if it was necessary to further prove this quality of our Savior's character."
"What a friend we have in Jesus, *All* our sins and griefs to bear." All our stupidity, all our blindness, all our stubbornness, and all our physical weakness We have seen in a previous chapter that being considerate of others is a part of true courage. In fact it is the very essence of love."

9. "Some authors who write for you and about you have wrongly judged you in this respect."

10. "He usually agrees with Mrs. Grundy, and Mrs. Grundy is often right in the check she puts upon behavior and speech." Mrs. Grundy is a minor character in Thomas Morton's play *Speed the Plough* (1798). She became in British literature an allusion to people who are extremely conventional.

11. Based upon the value of silver in 2014.

12. Author unknown

13. "He is: 'Closer to you than breathing, Nearer than hands and feet."

14. Author unknown

15. "A person without tact that comes to mind in a recent fiction novel is, Mr. Gradgrind. He is always so sure of himself. To him, the only thing that matters is reason and facts. He believes he is right about everything and smugly dismisses the

opinions of others without even consideration." Mr. Thomas Gradgrind is the headmaster in Charles Dickens' novel, *Hard Times*. "Gradrind" is a metaphor to describe an unfriendly person who is only interested with facts and figures.

16. It was Charles Dickens' character, Mrs. Gummidge who always said, "I feels it more than others."

17. Joan of Arc (ca. 1412 – 30 May 1431) was burned at the stake at the age of 19 and is considered a martyr by the Roman Catholic church. Marie-Anne Charlotte de Corday d'Armont was a figure in the French Revolution who died by the guillotine.

Printed in Great Britain
by Amazon.co.uk, Ltd.,
Marston Gate.